Gallery

Grim Disclaimer

All characters appearing in this work are fictitious. Any resemblance to real persons, living or dead, is purely coincidental. (Or is it)

Thanks To: Leah C., Britney C., Brittany V., DJ, Heather N, Brennen S, Pat, Leah (second mom) Amber M., Kristy (my 6th grade teacher), Andrew and Don H., my family, Stephanie K. and O, Brittany K., my cousin Jennifer who without her help this wouldn't be seen today. Dom, Michael, and John, Josh Murphy, Mama Poole and John P.

Moms + sisters

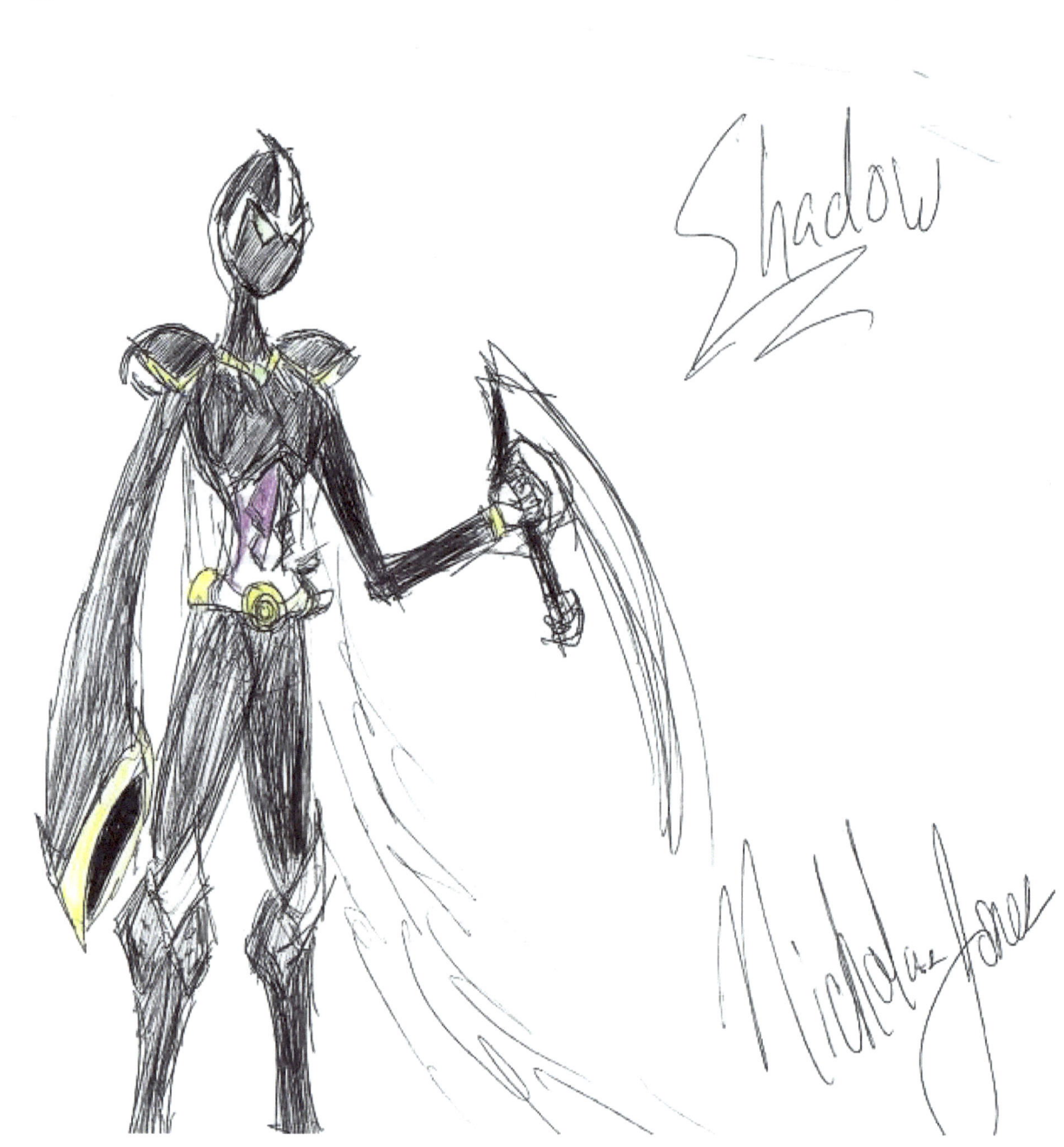

Shadow

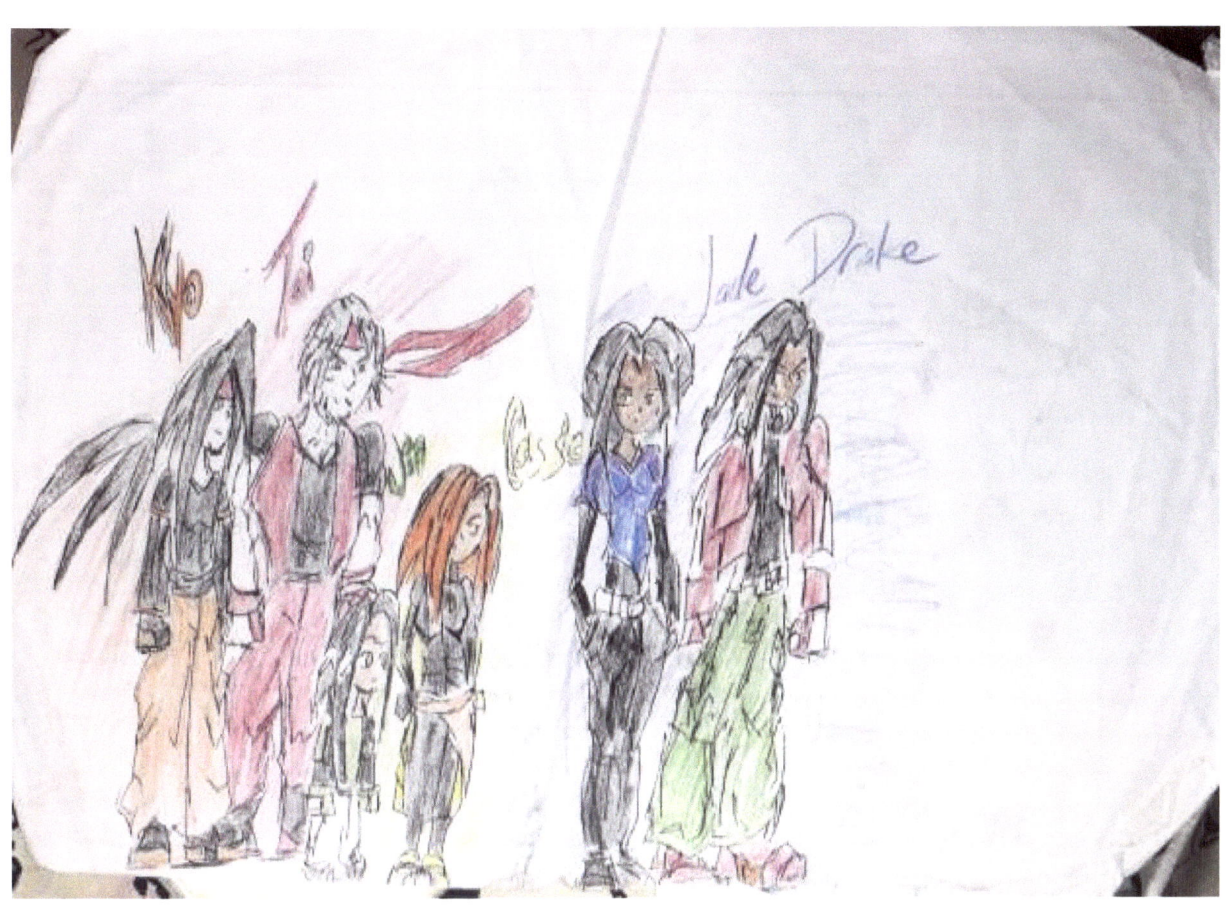

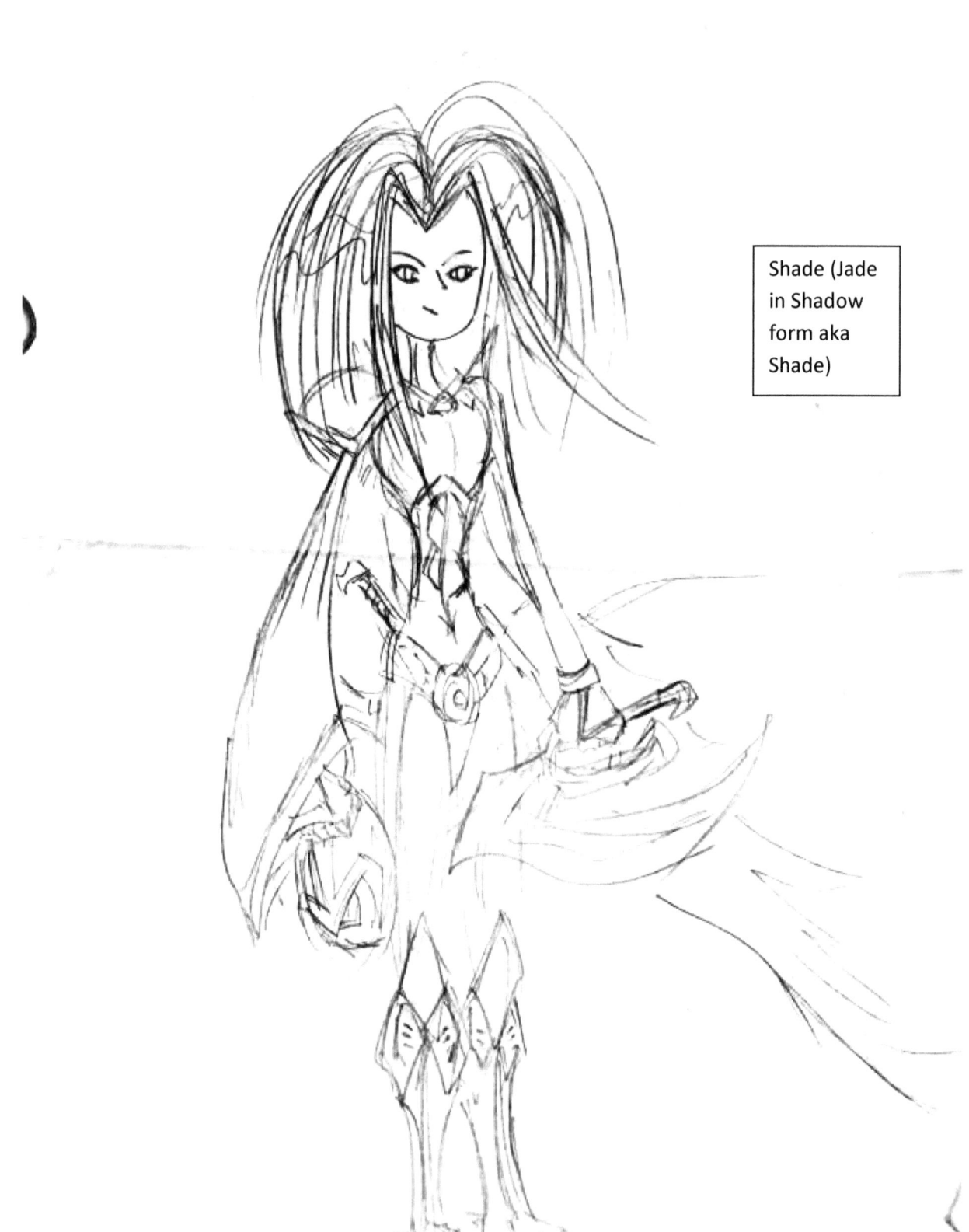

Shade (Jade in Shadow form aka Shade)

Jade

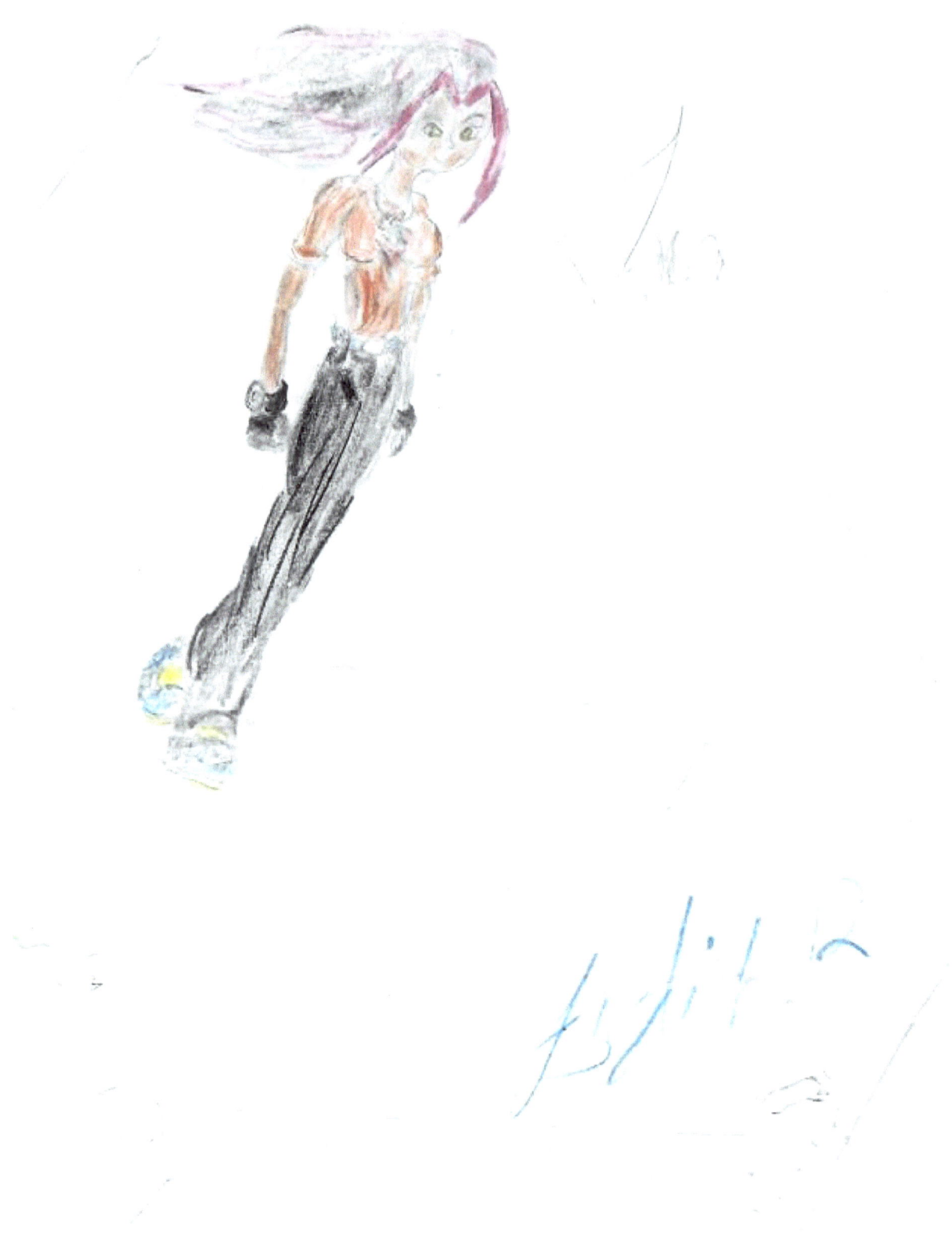

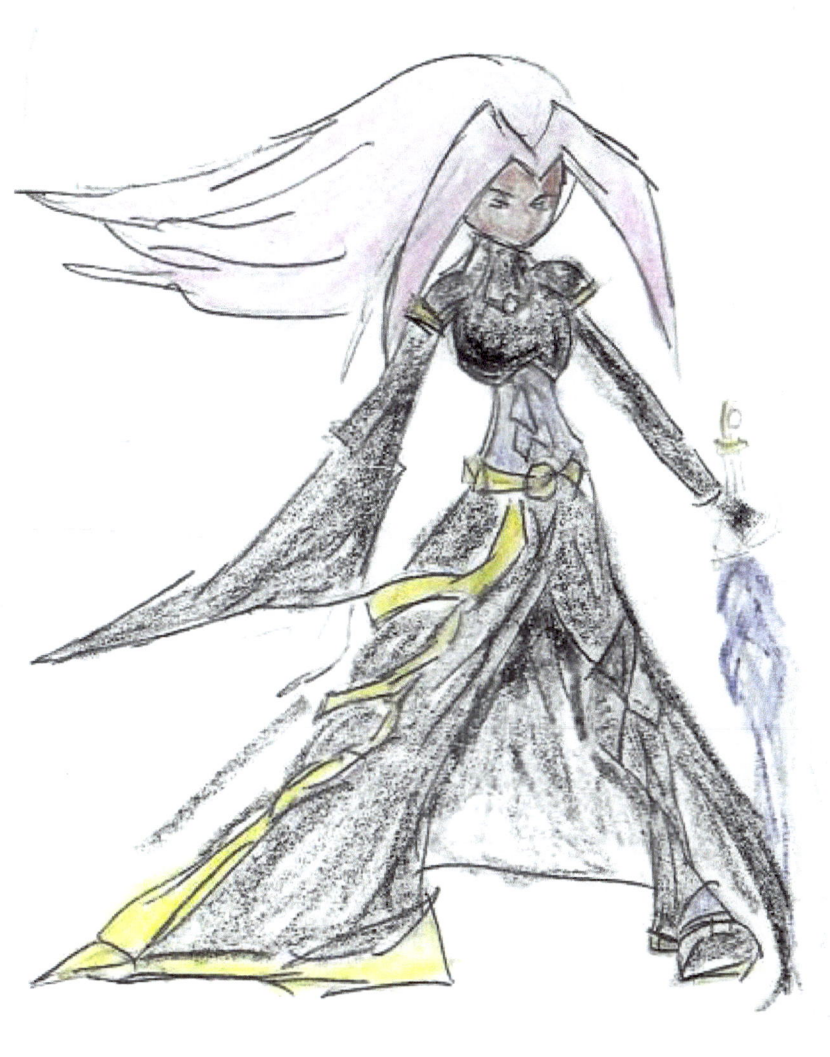

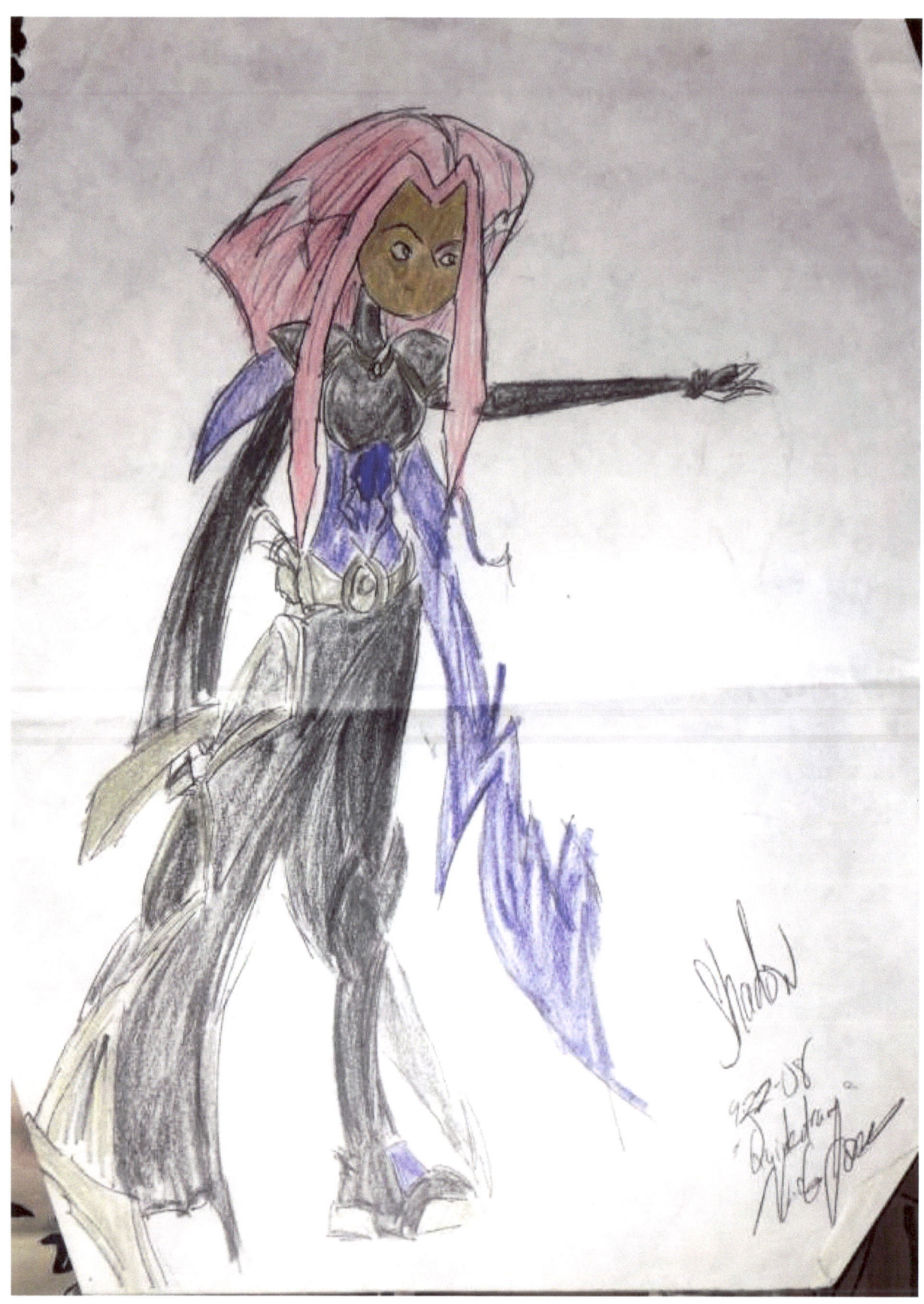

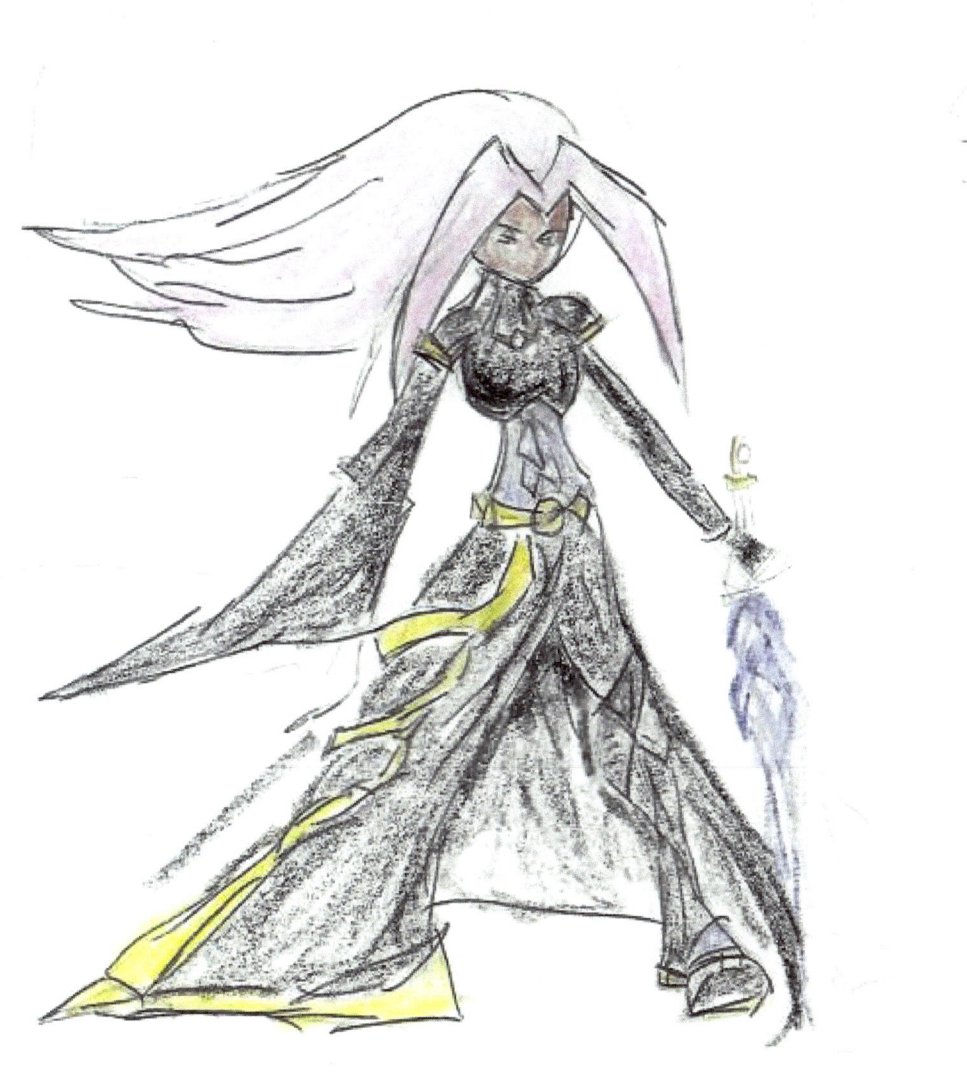

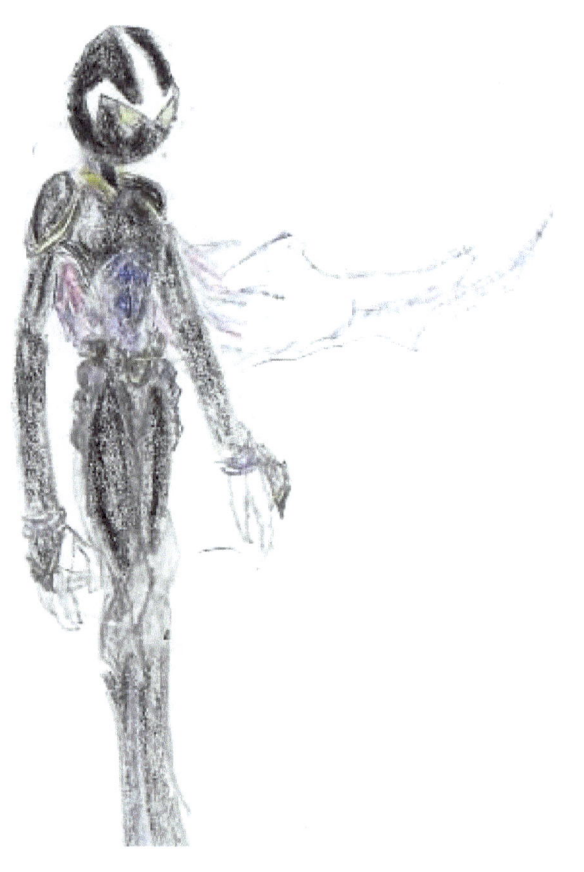

Jade's Shadow variant

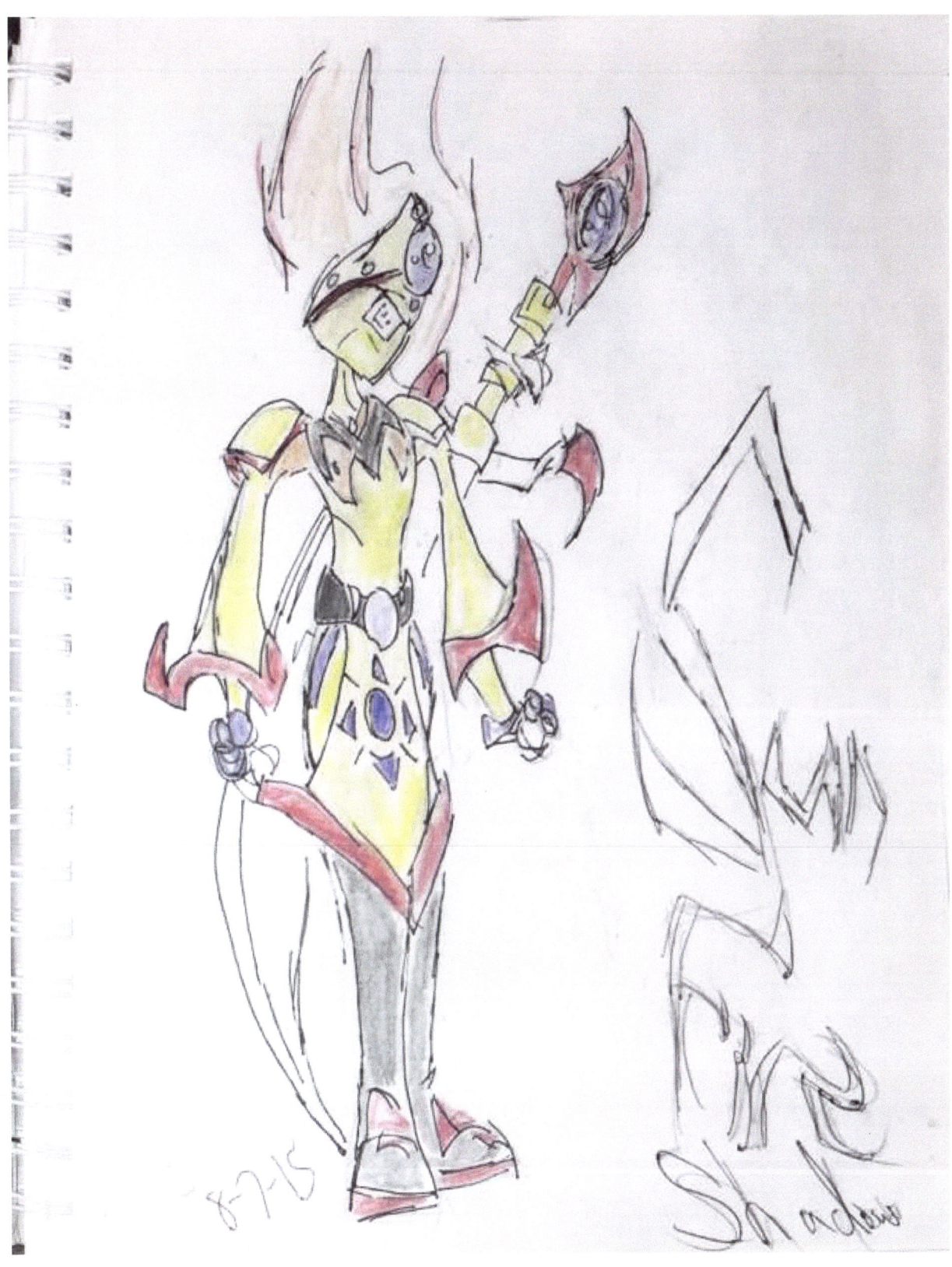

Sunfire Shadow (Cassandra)

Chibis

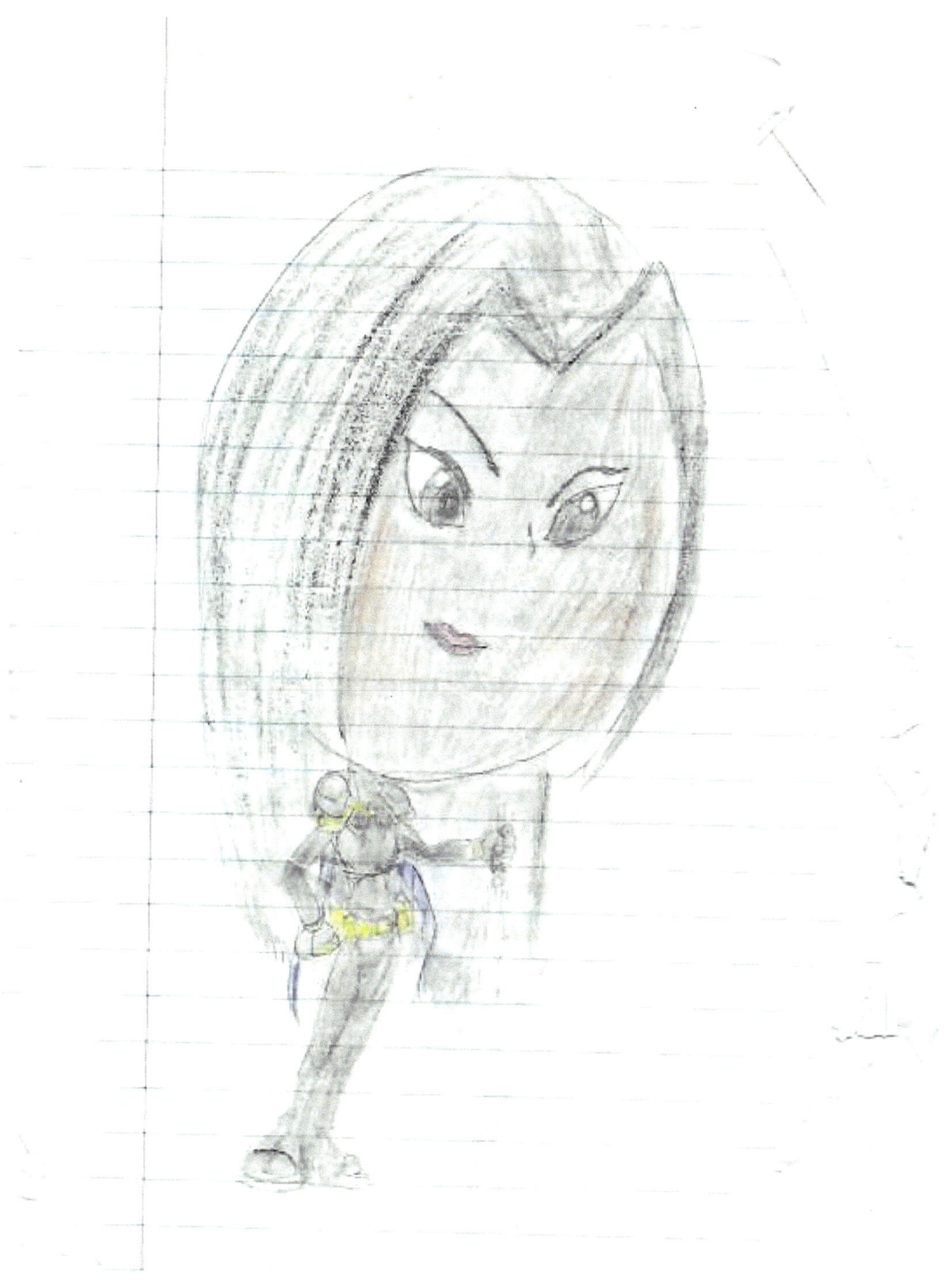

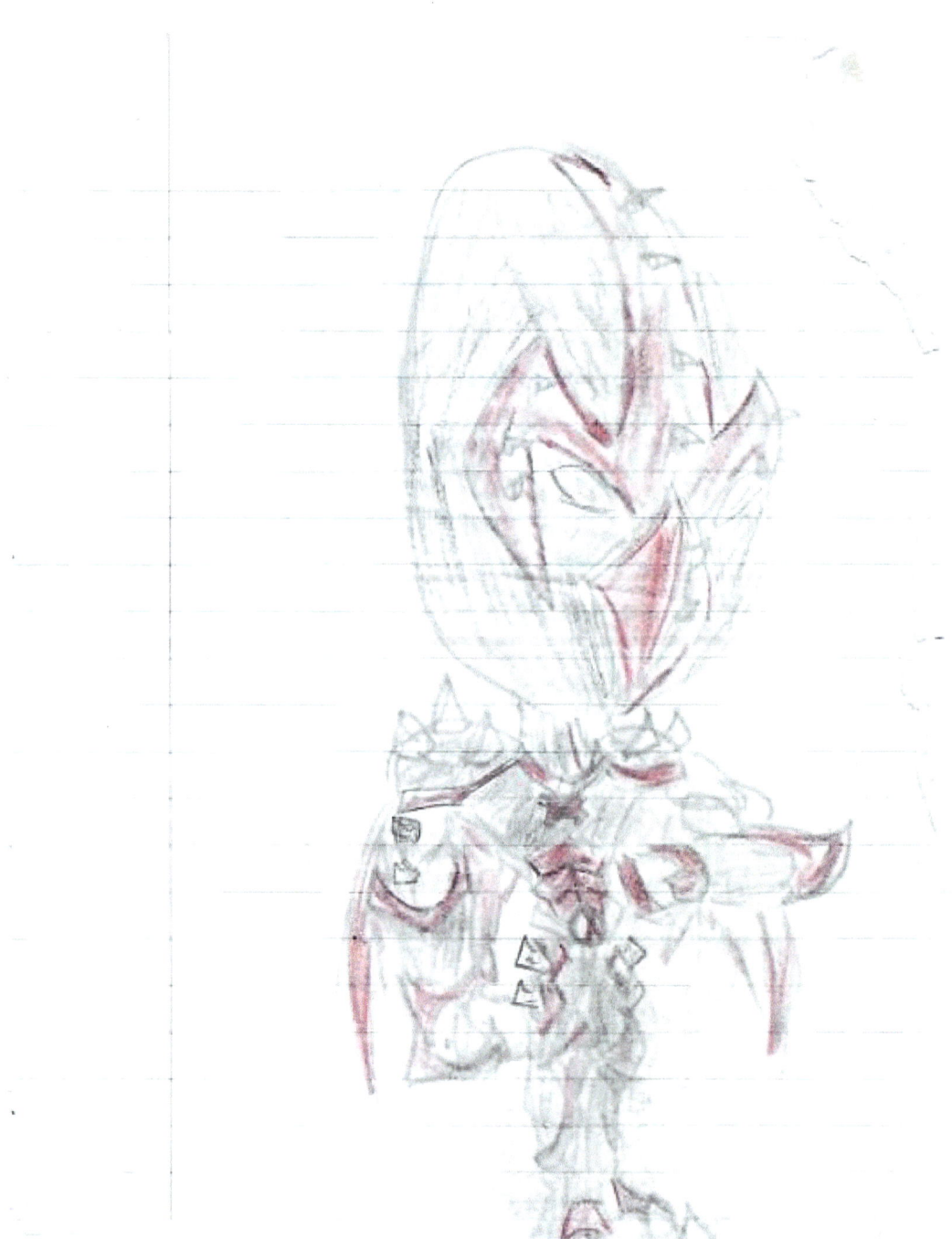

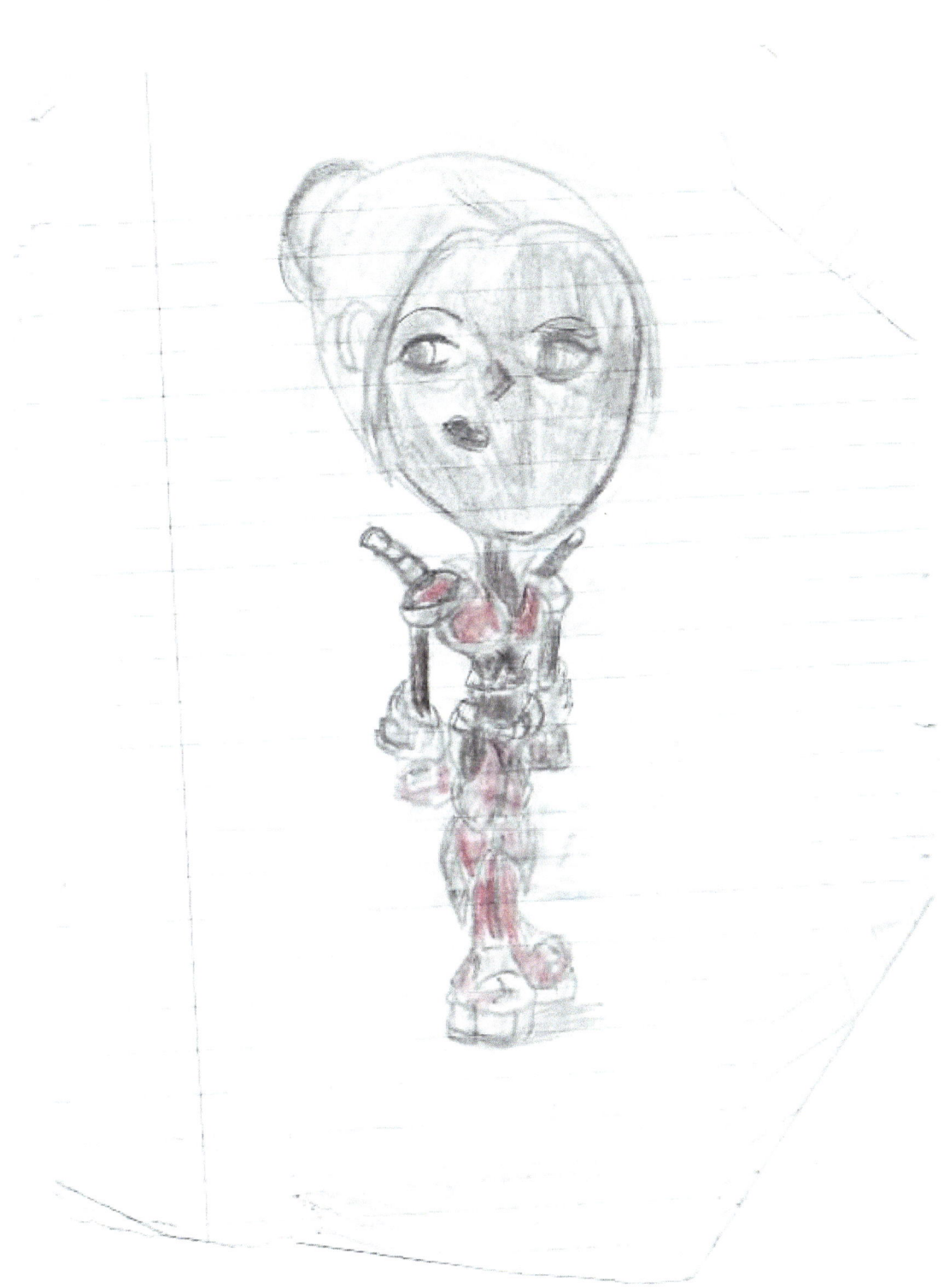

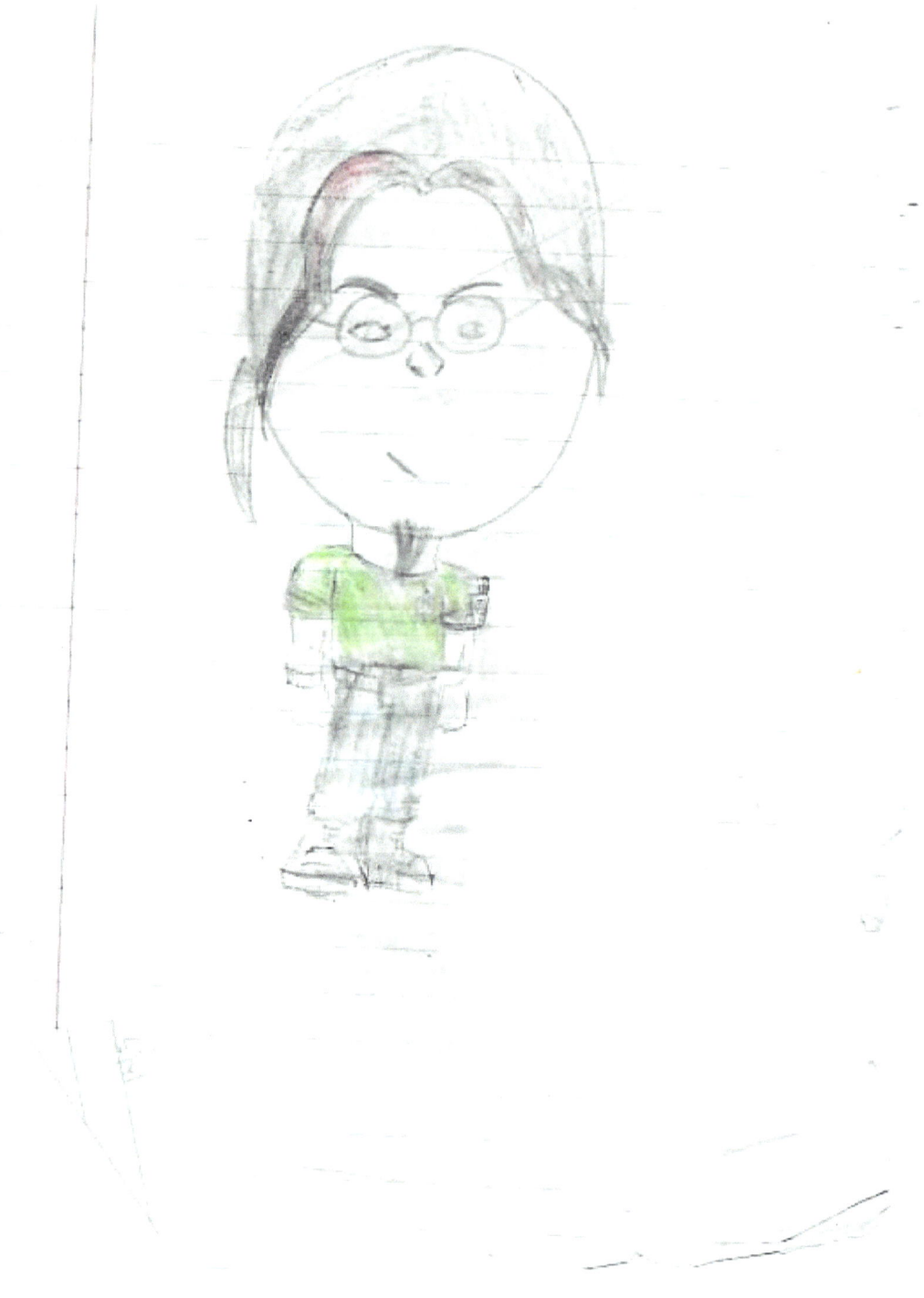

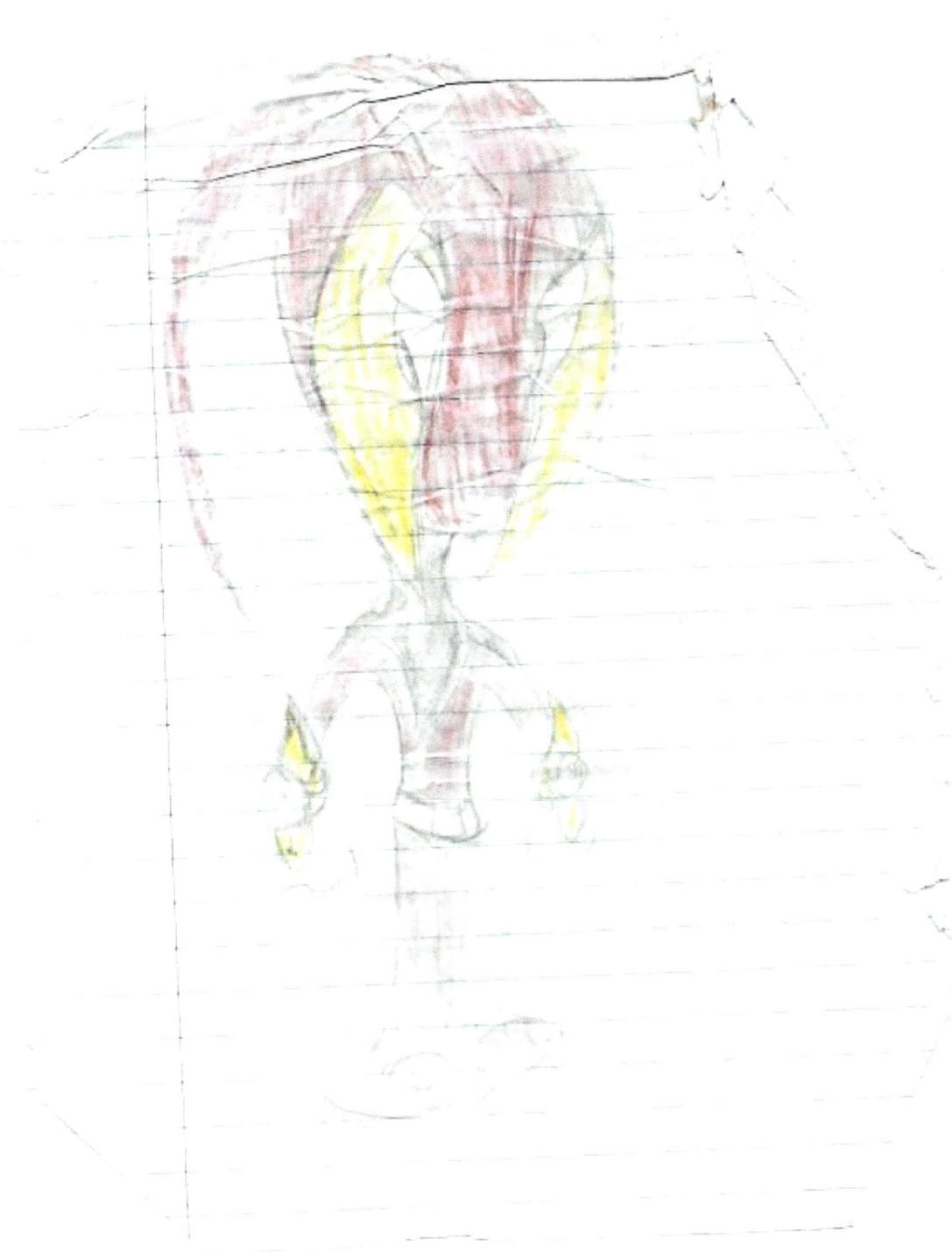

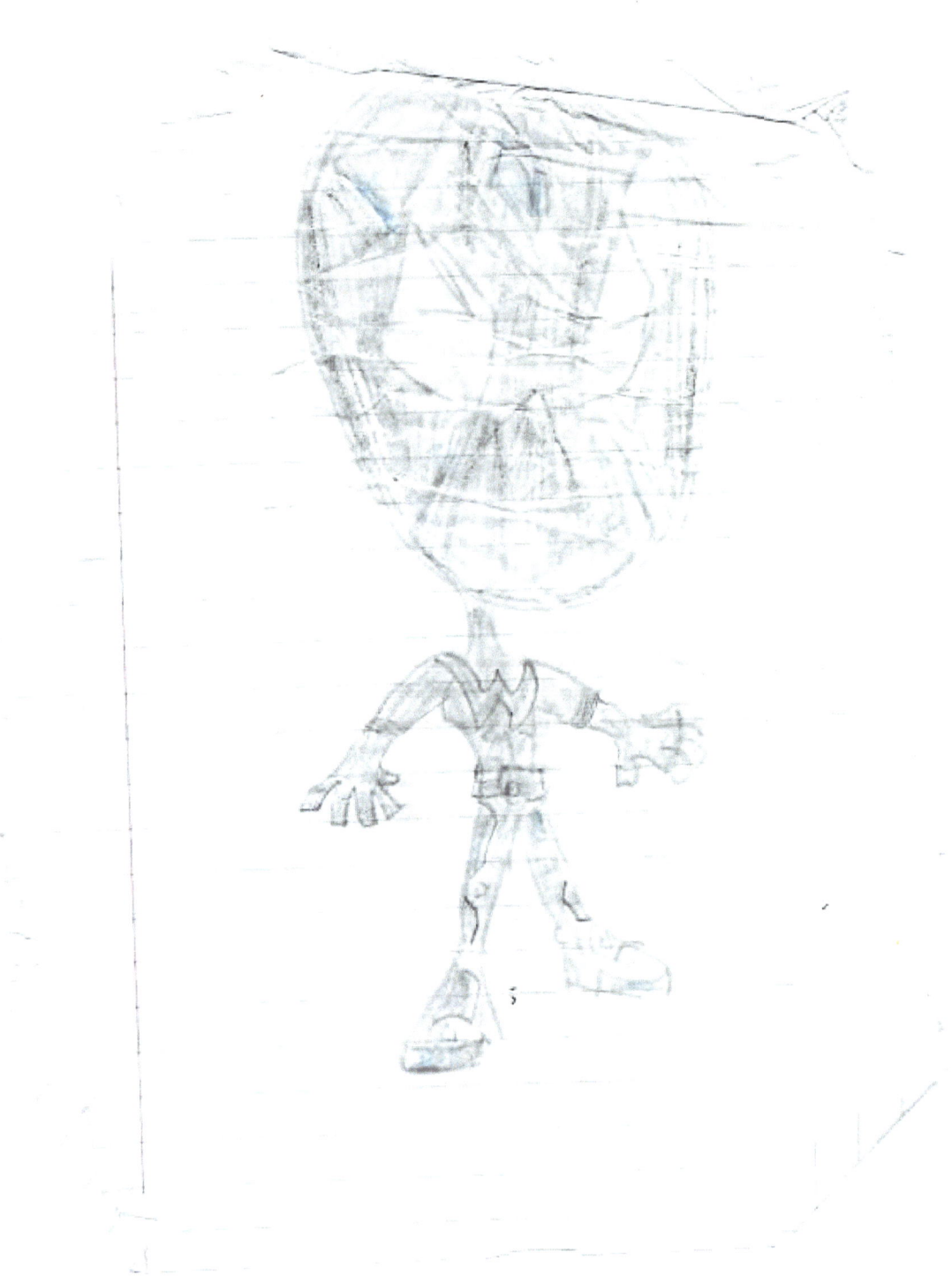

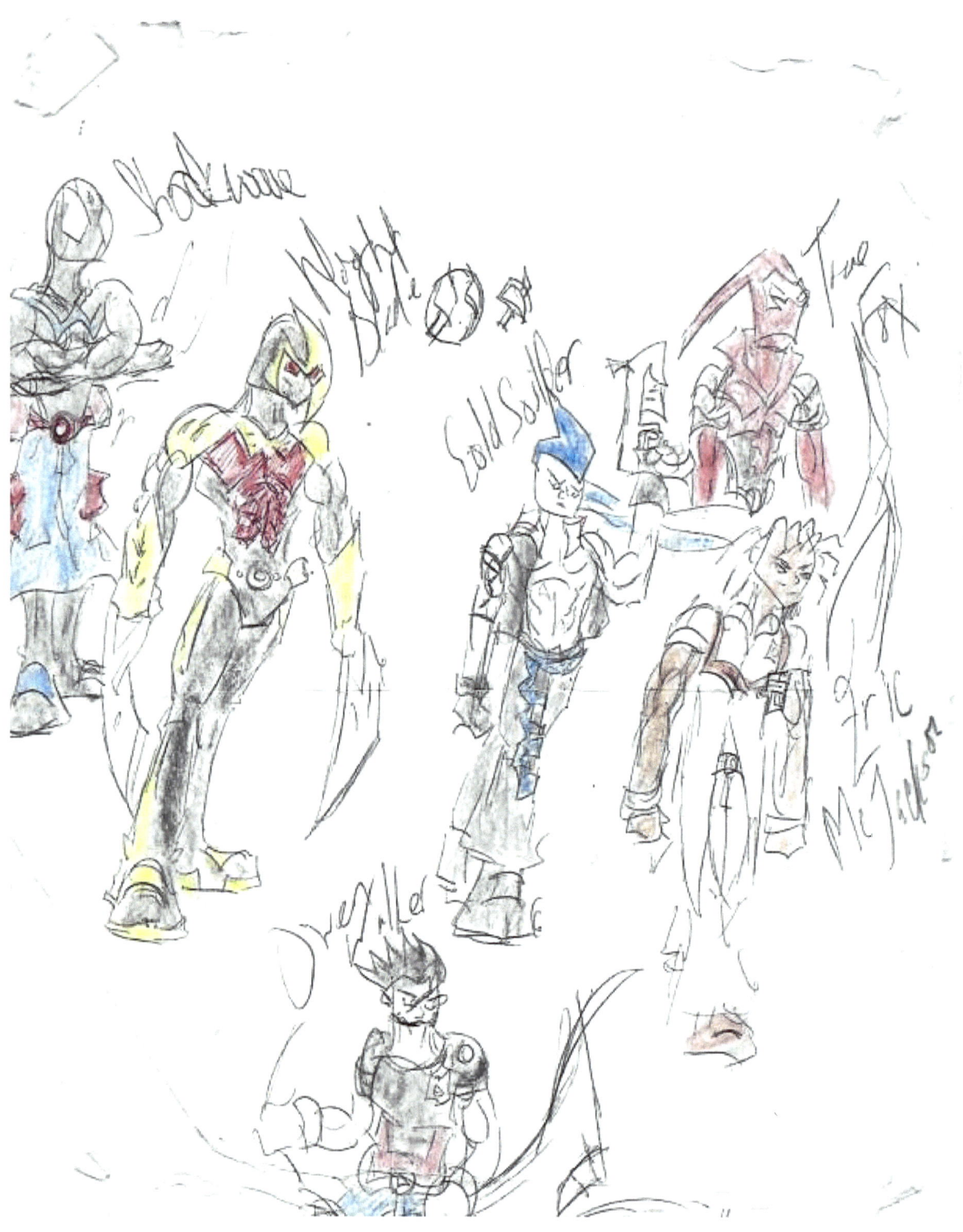

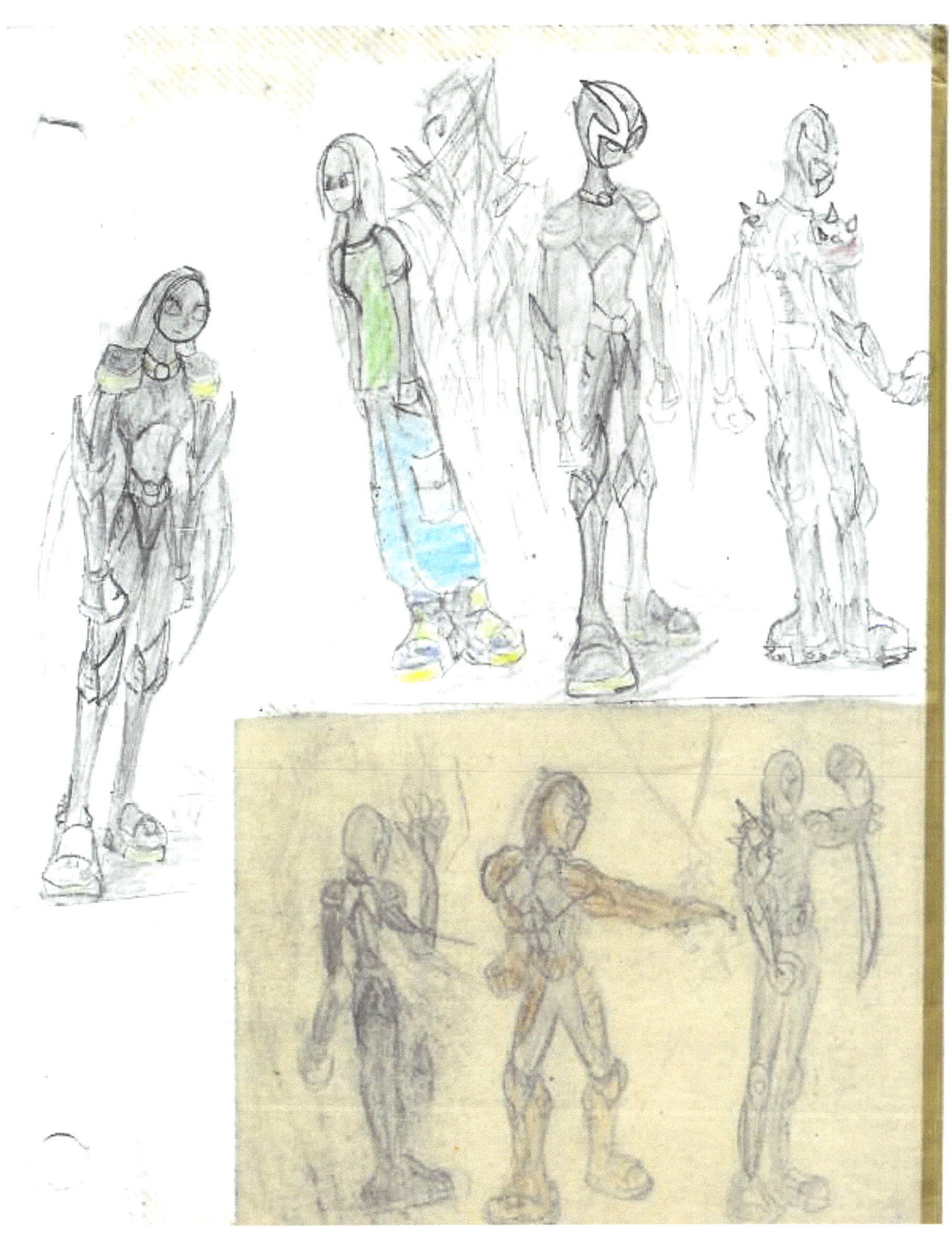

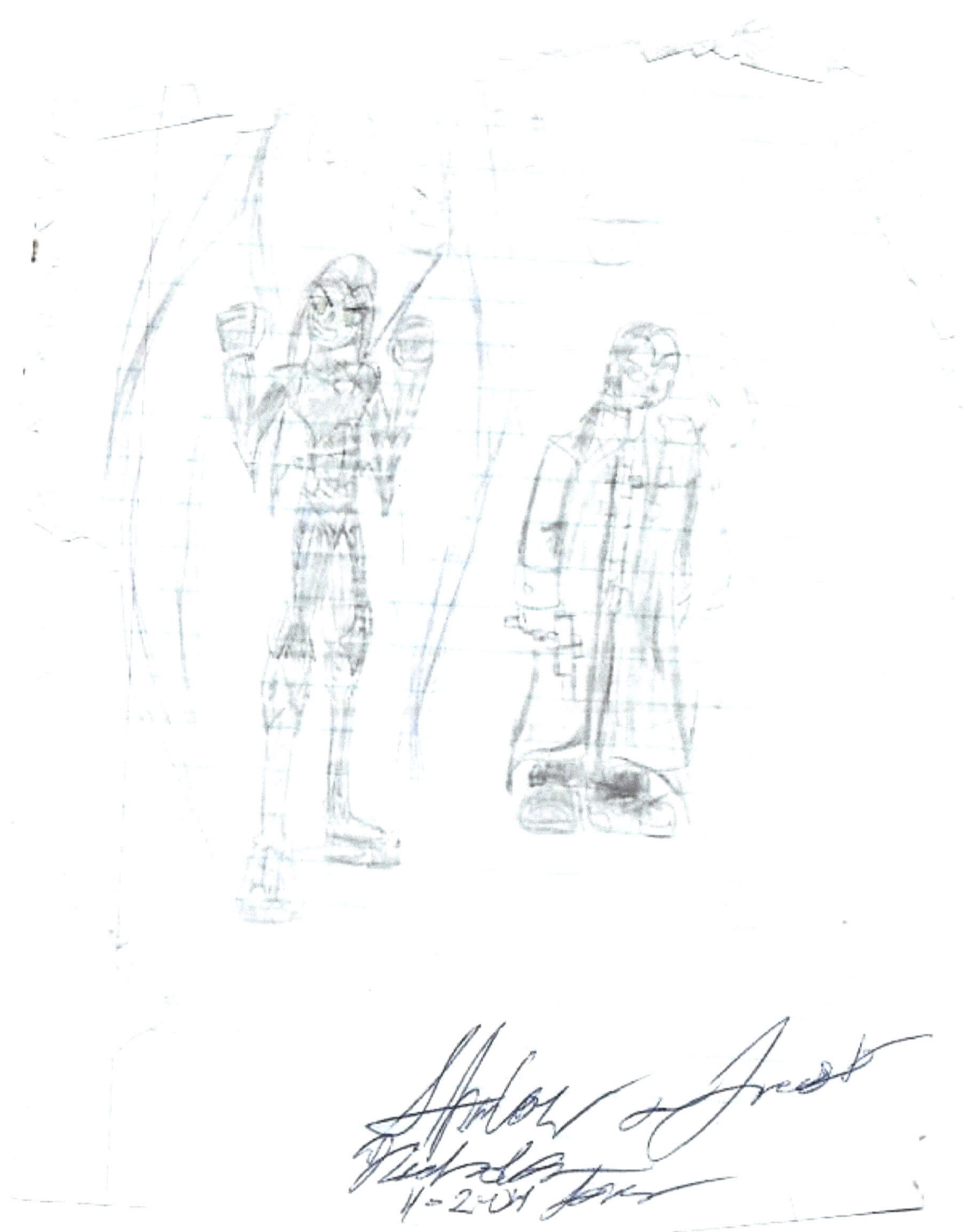

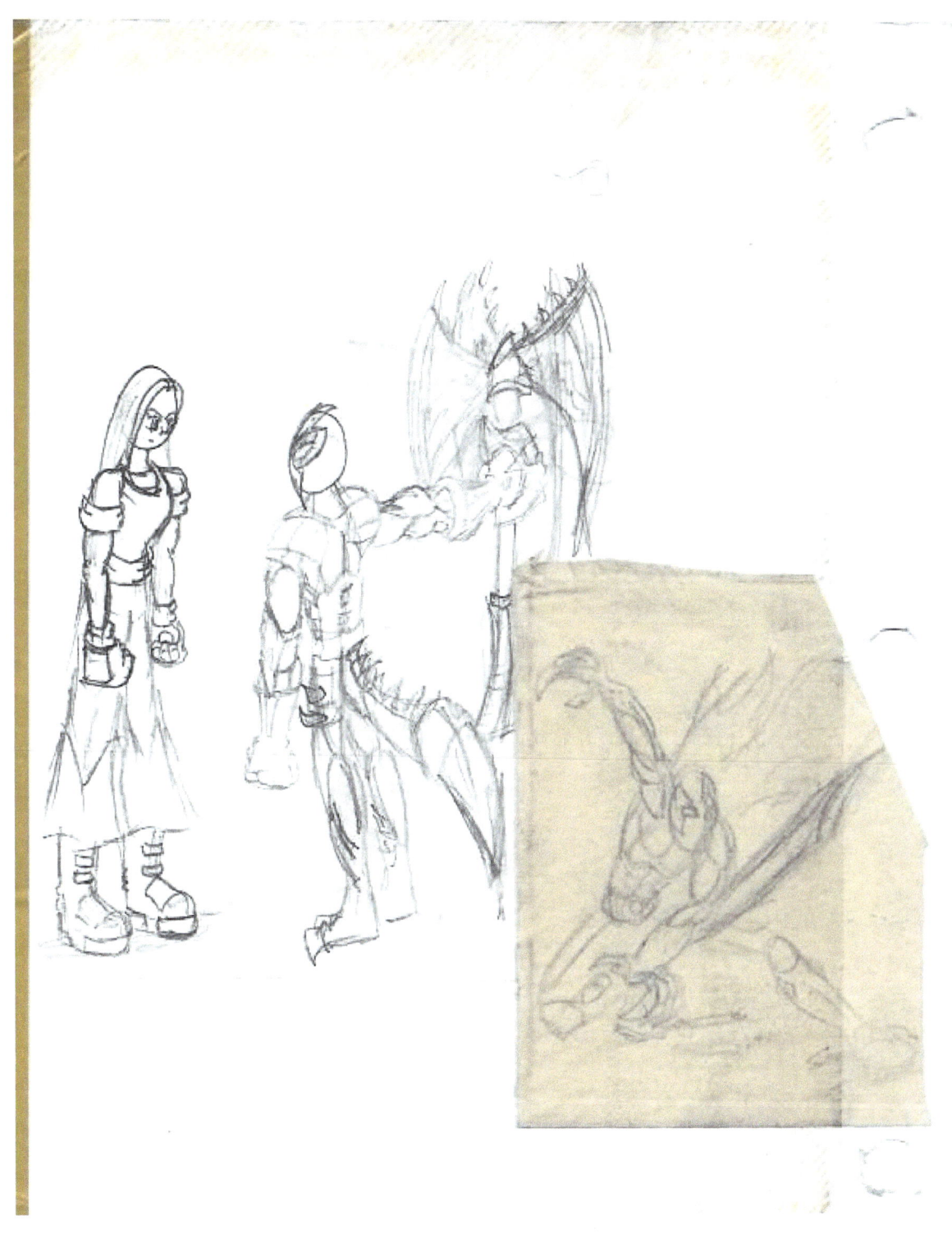

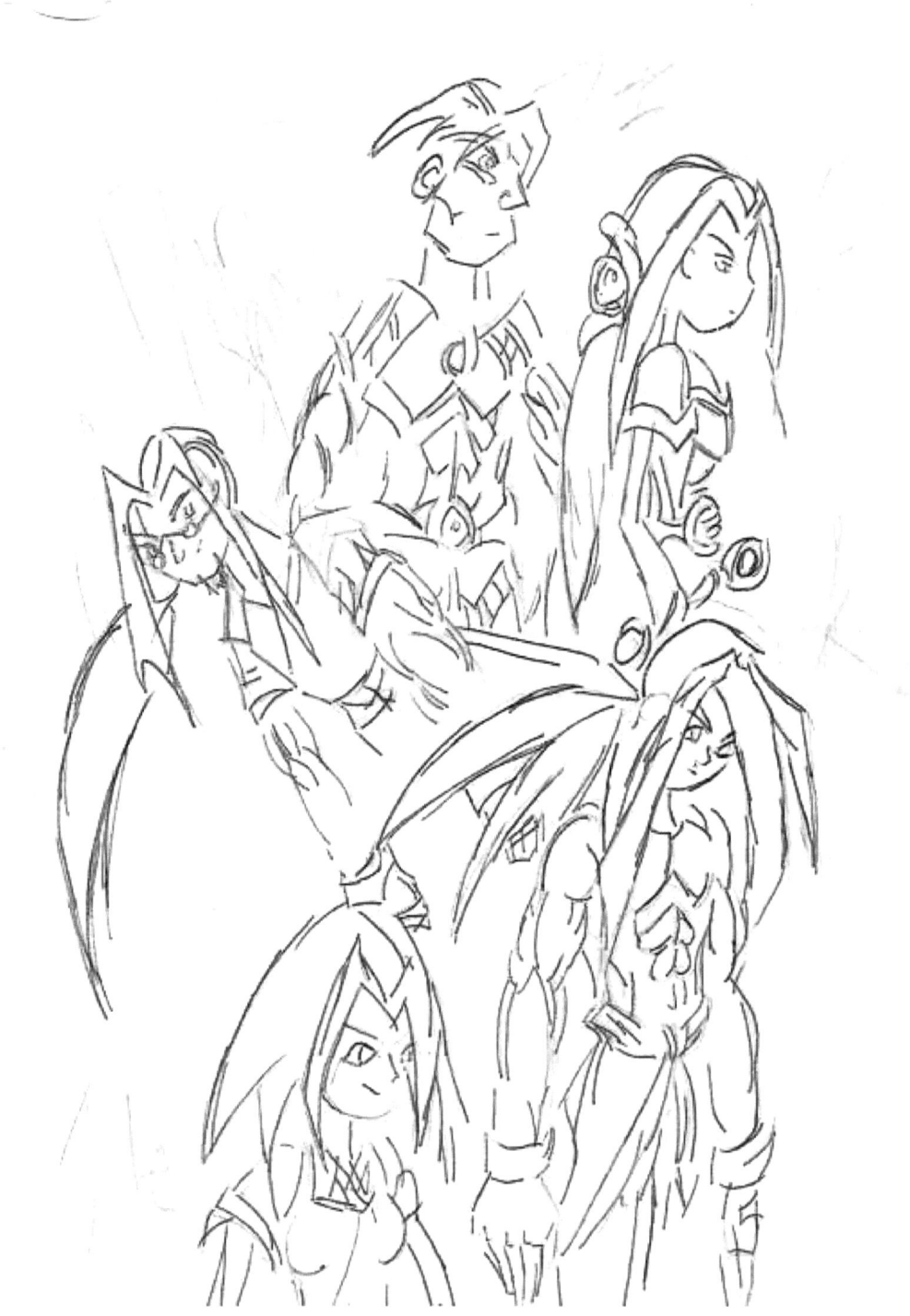

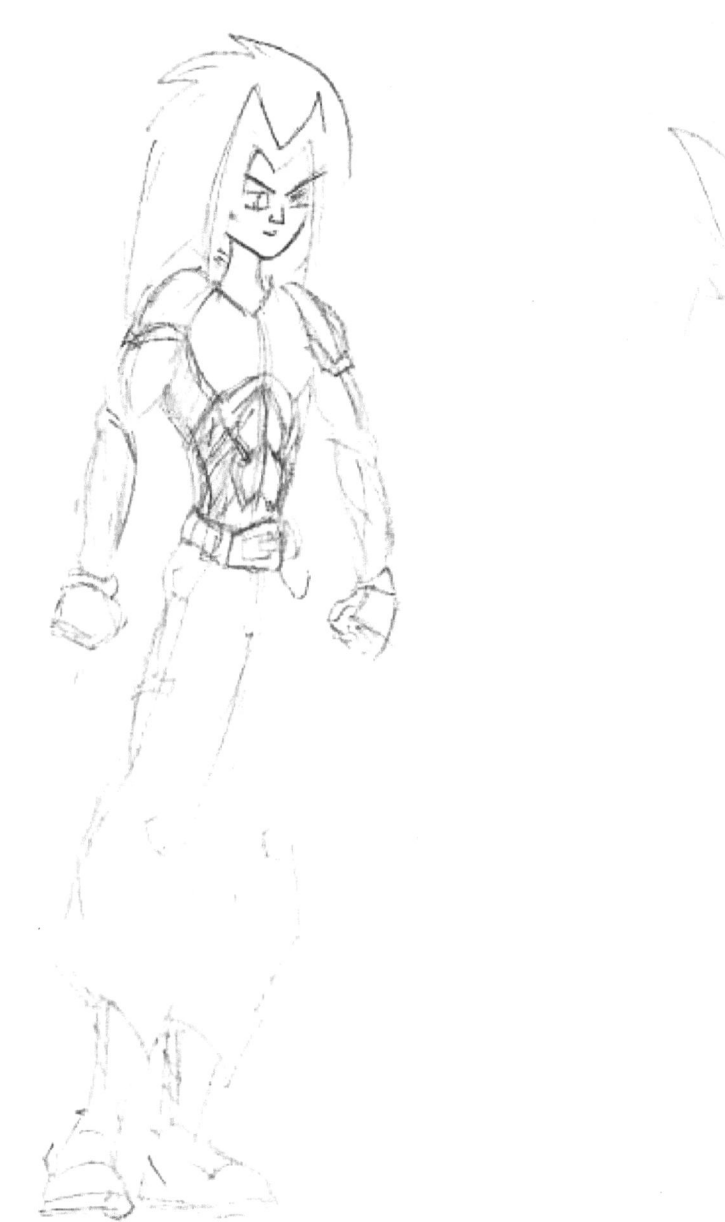

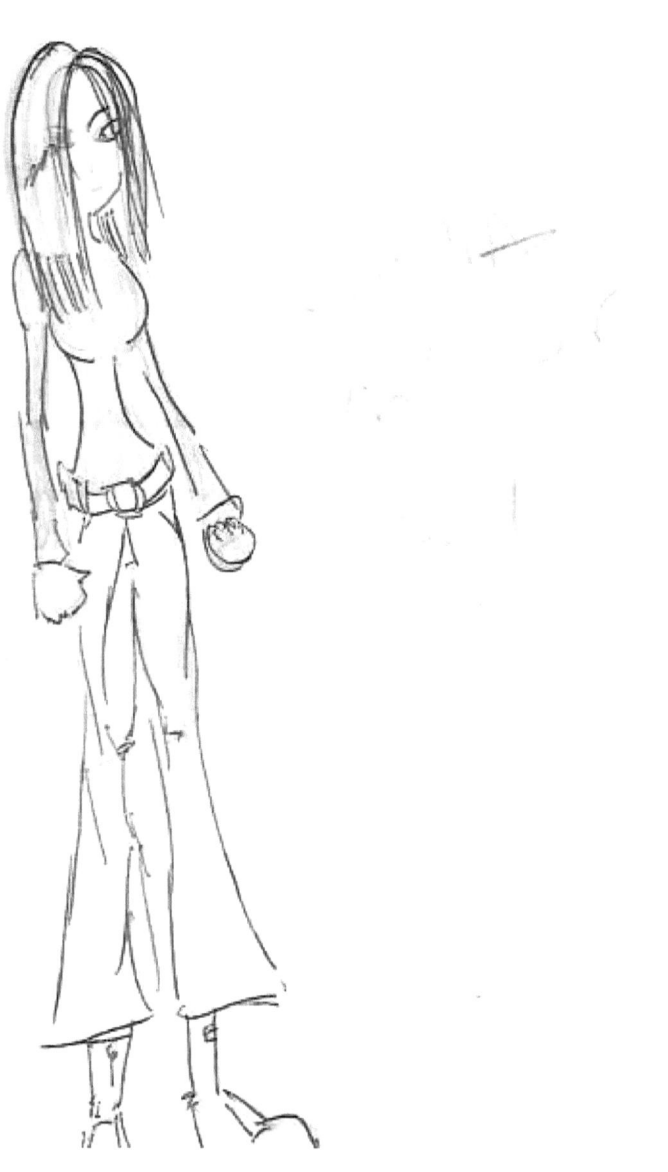

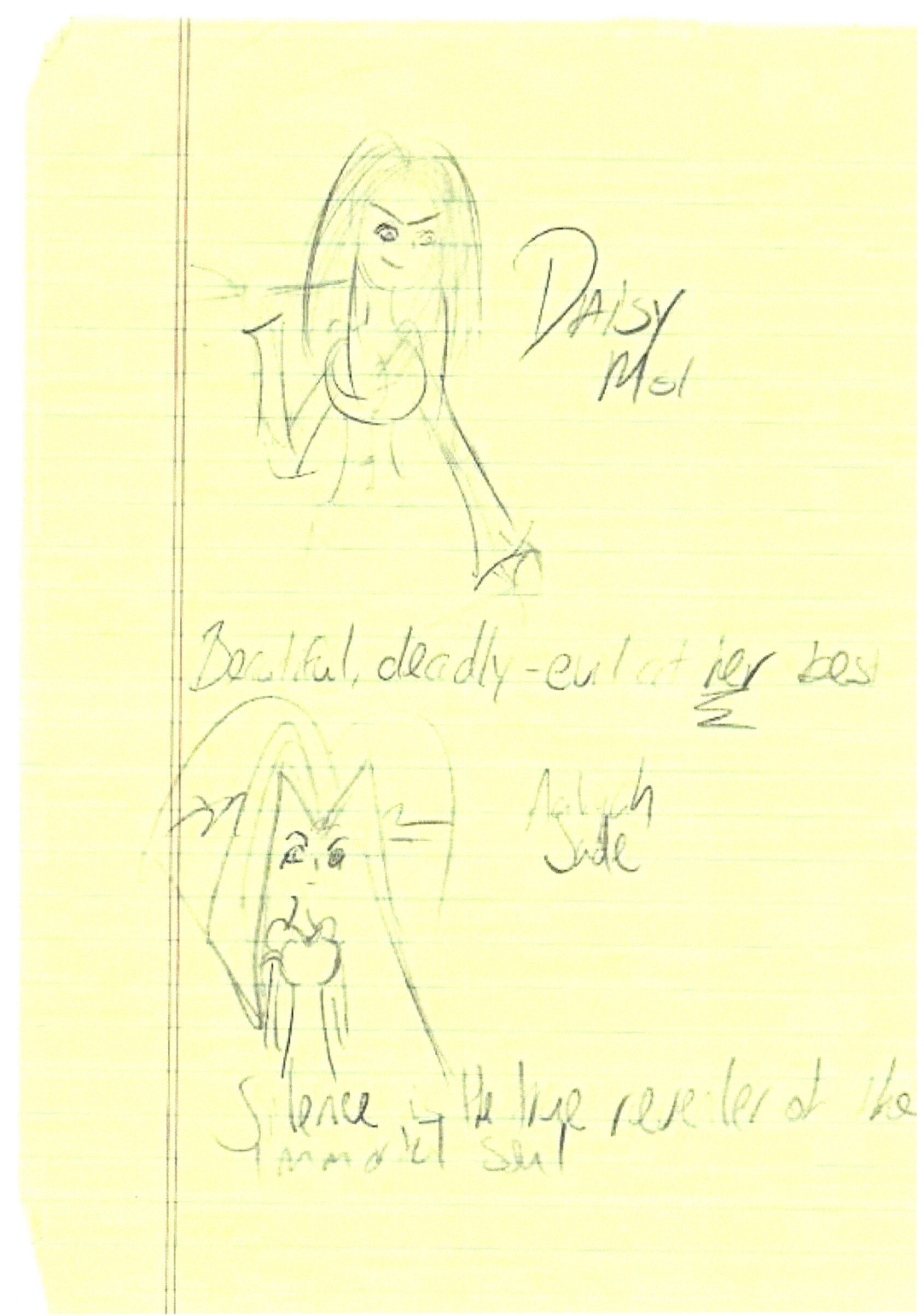

Daisy Mol

Beautiful, deadly - evil at her best

Analych
Side

Silence is the true reveiler of the
immortal soul

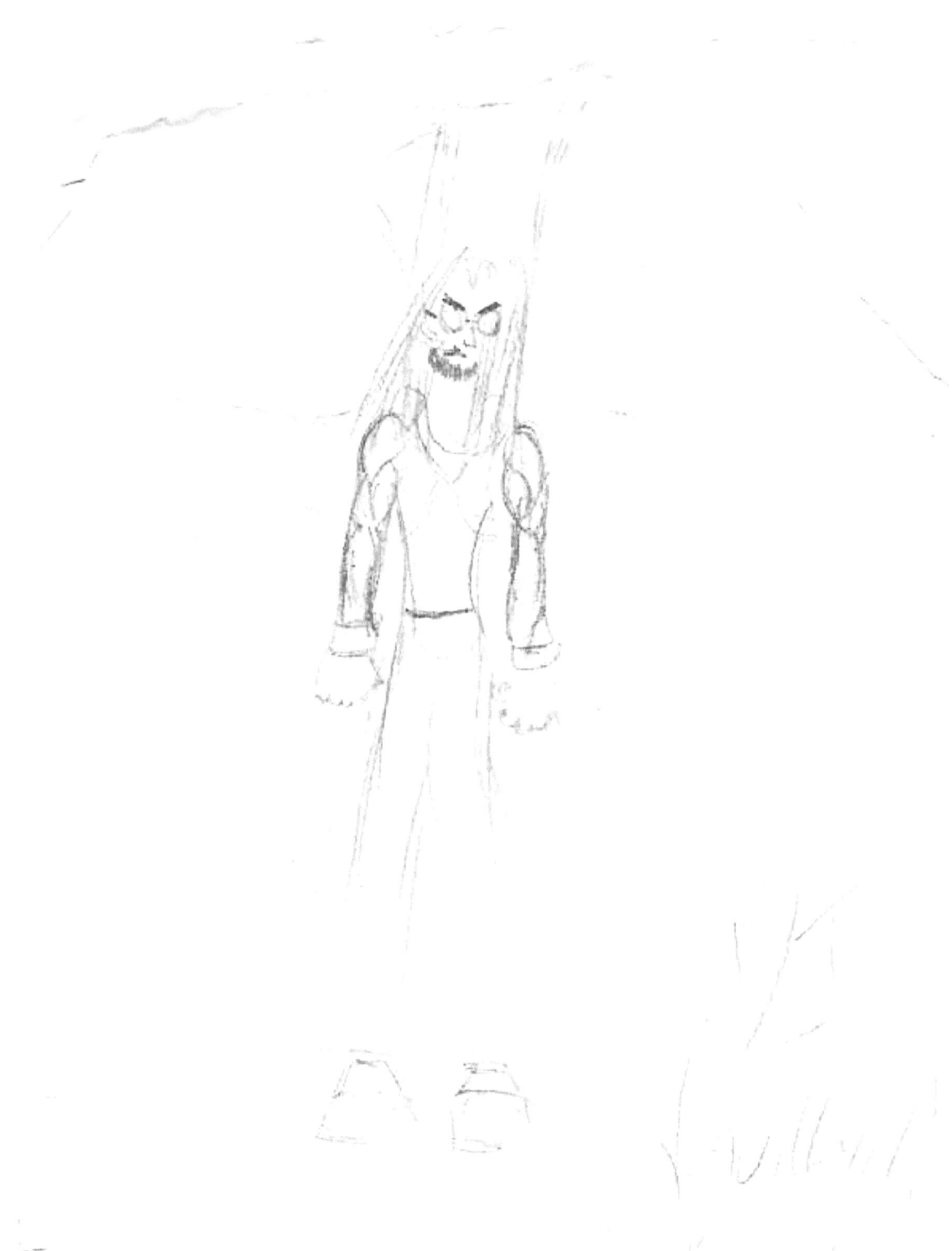

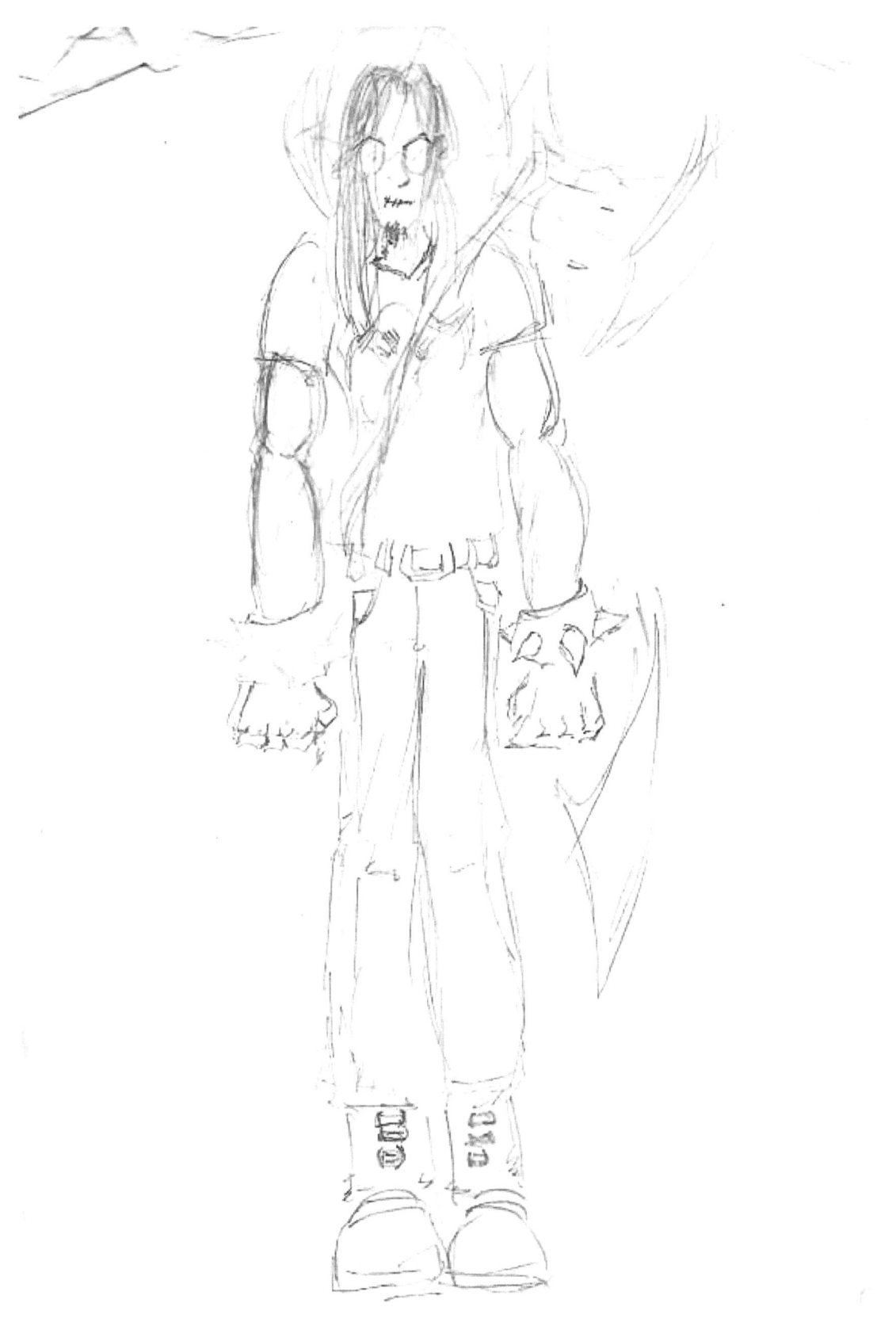

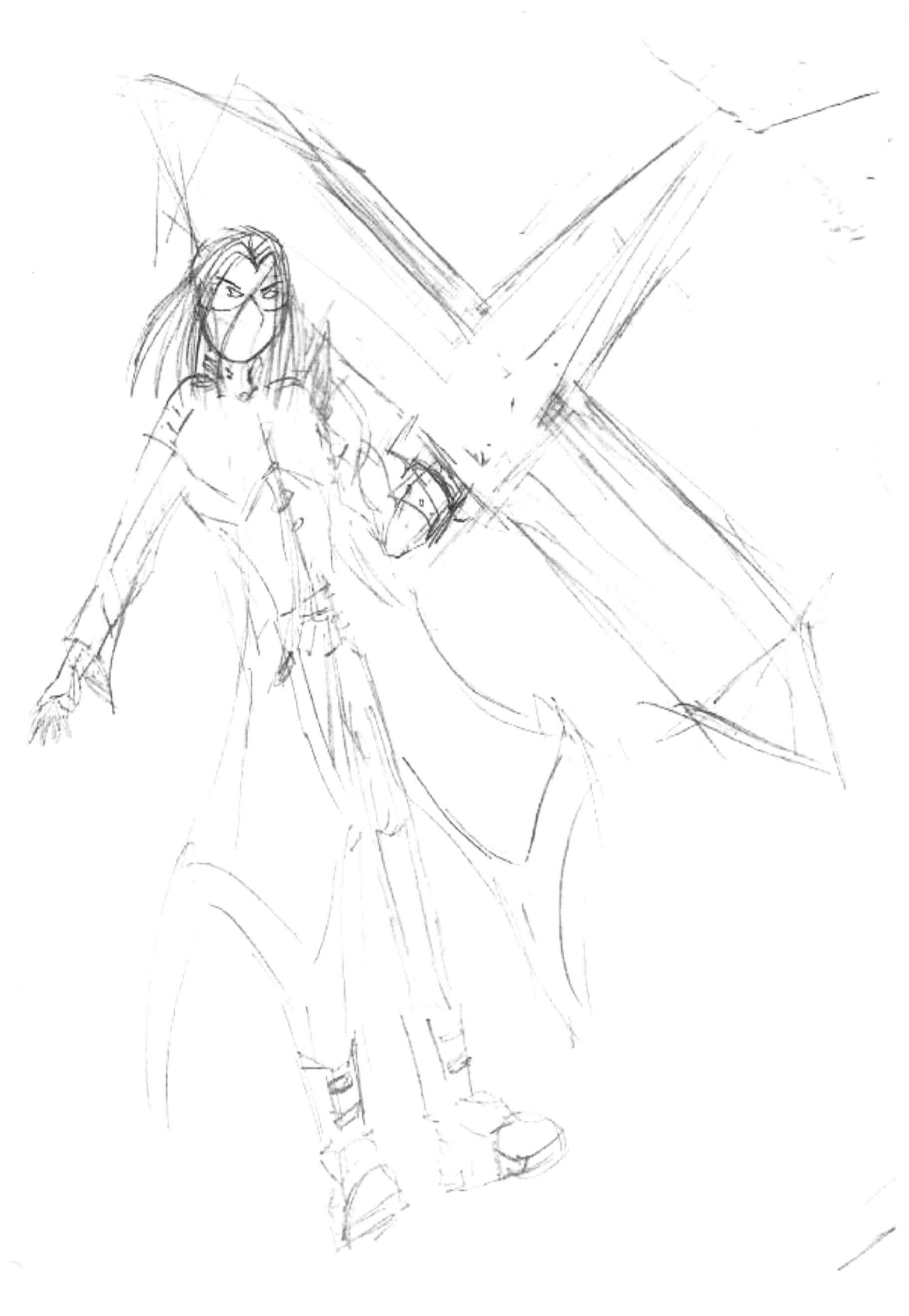

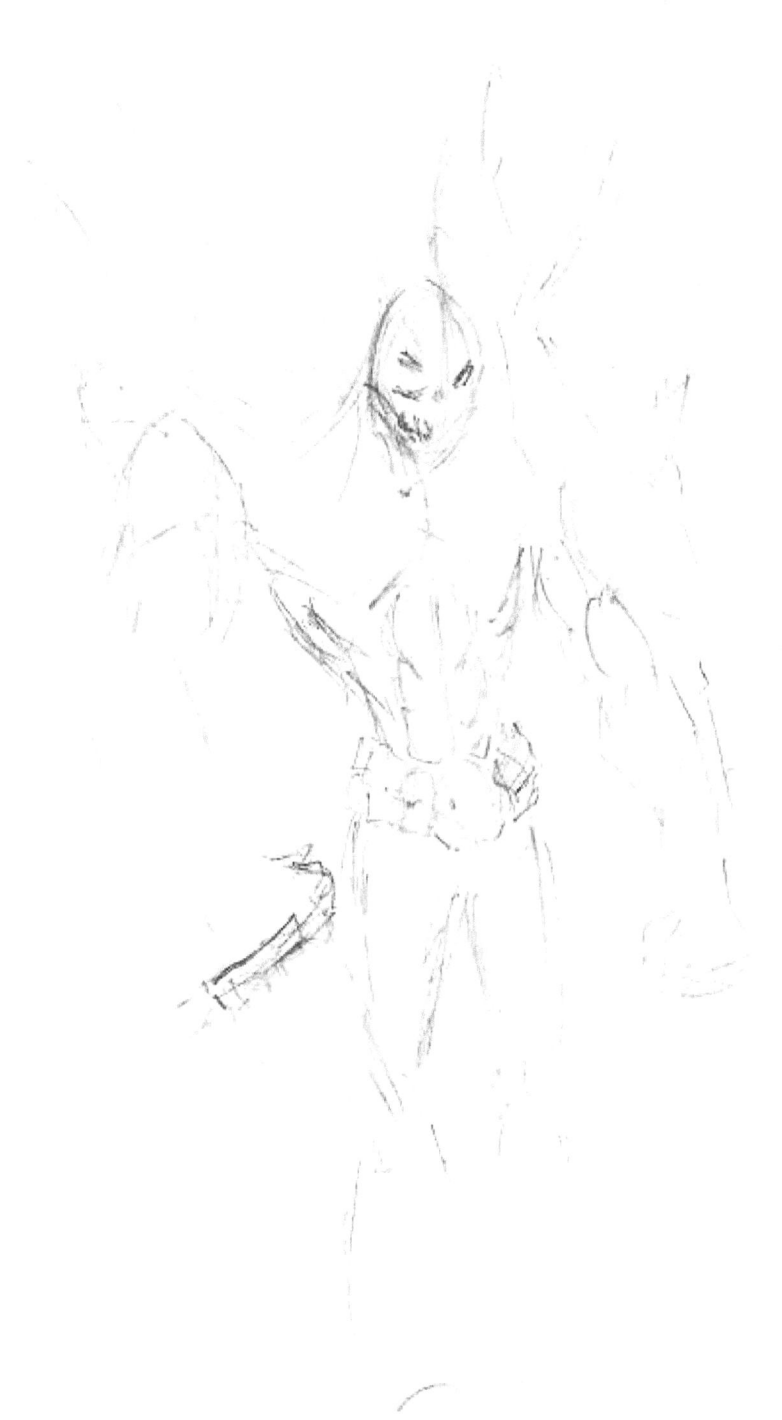

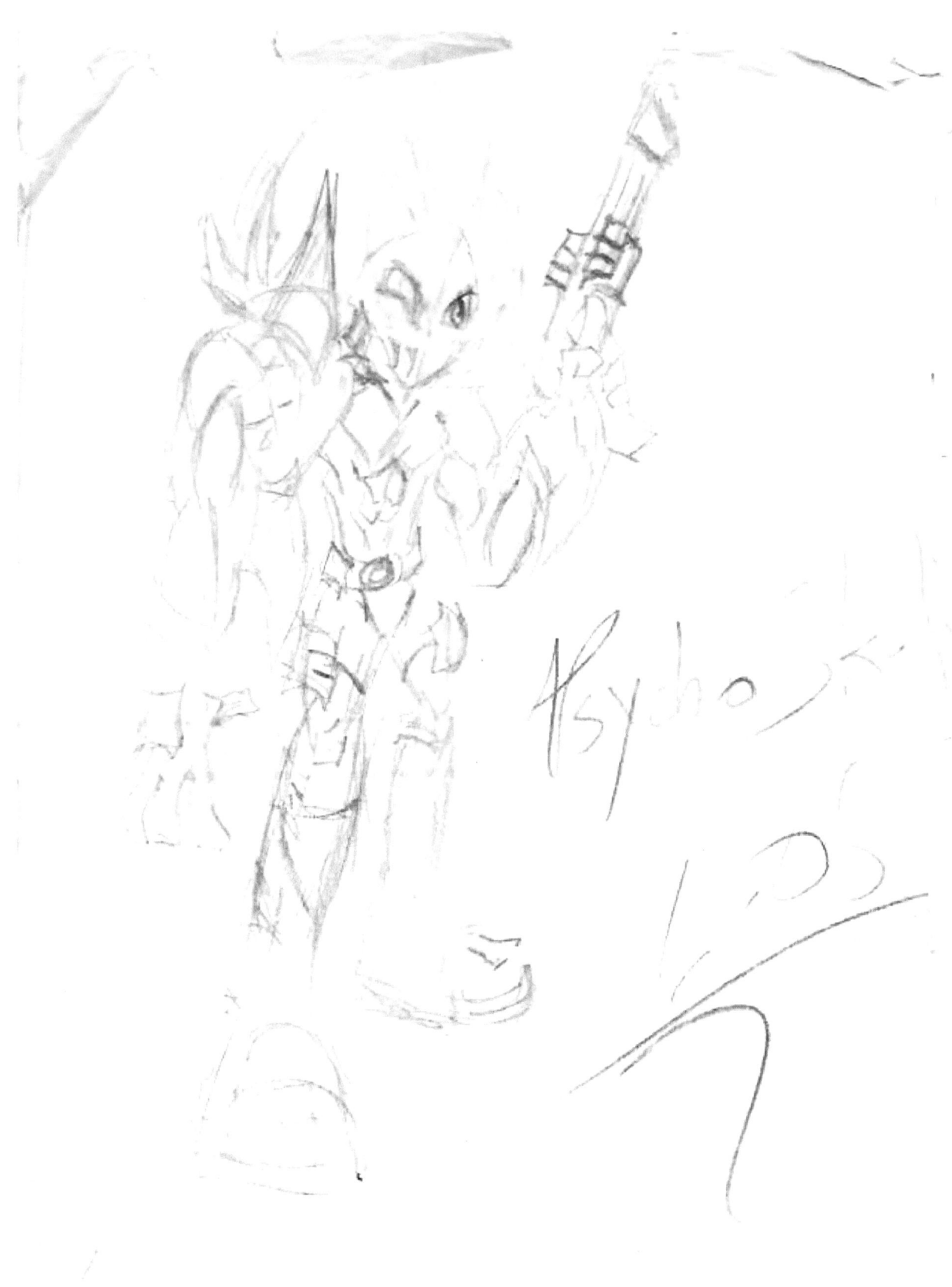

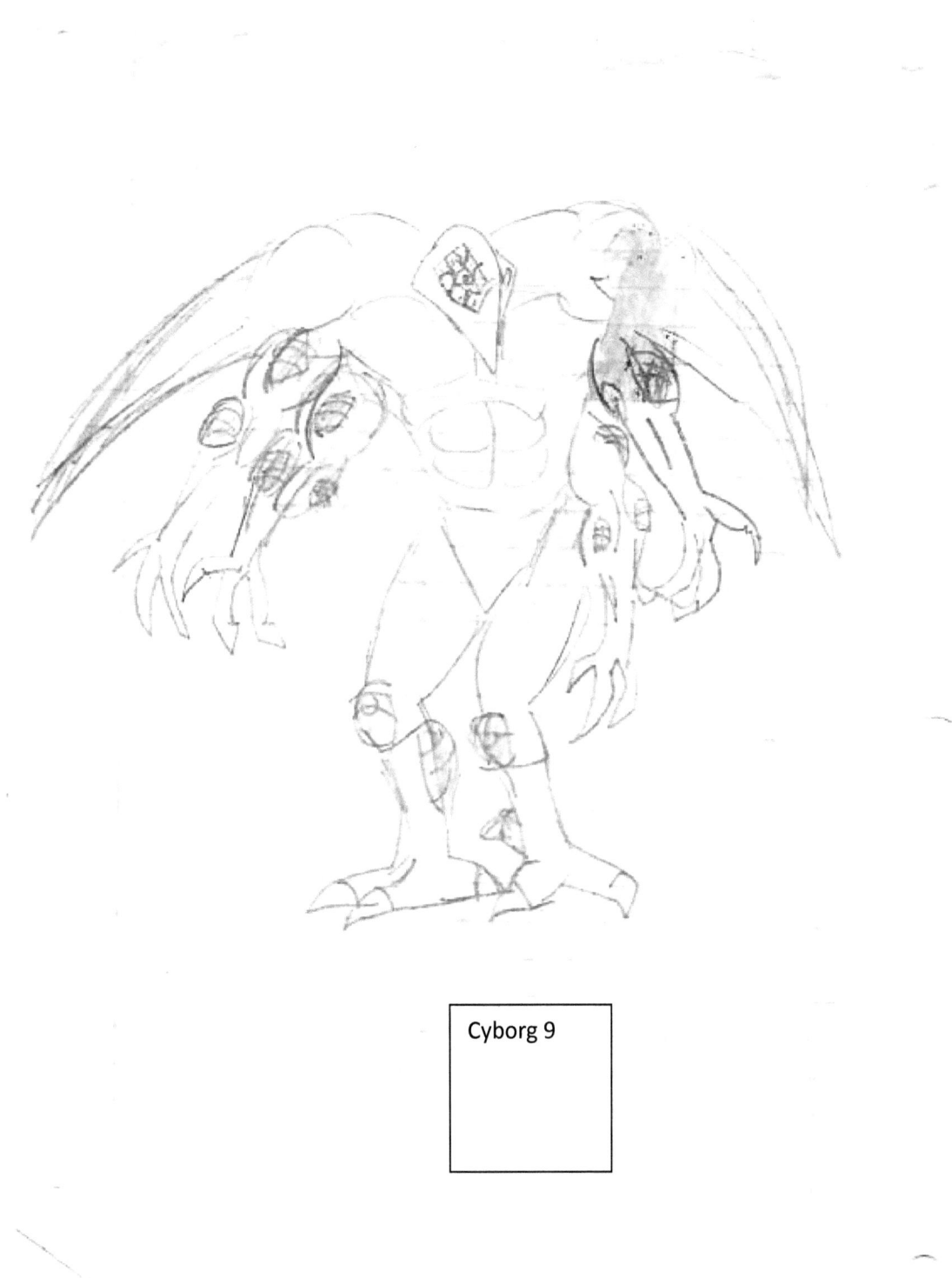

Cyborg 9

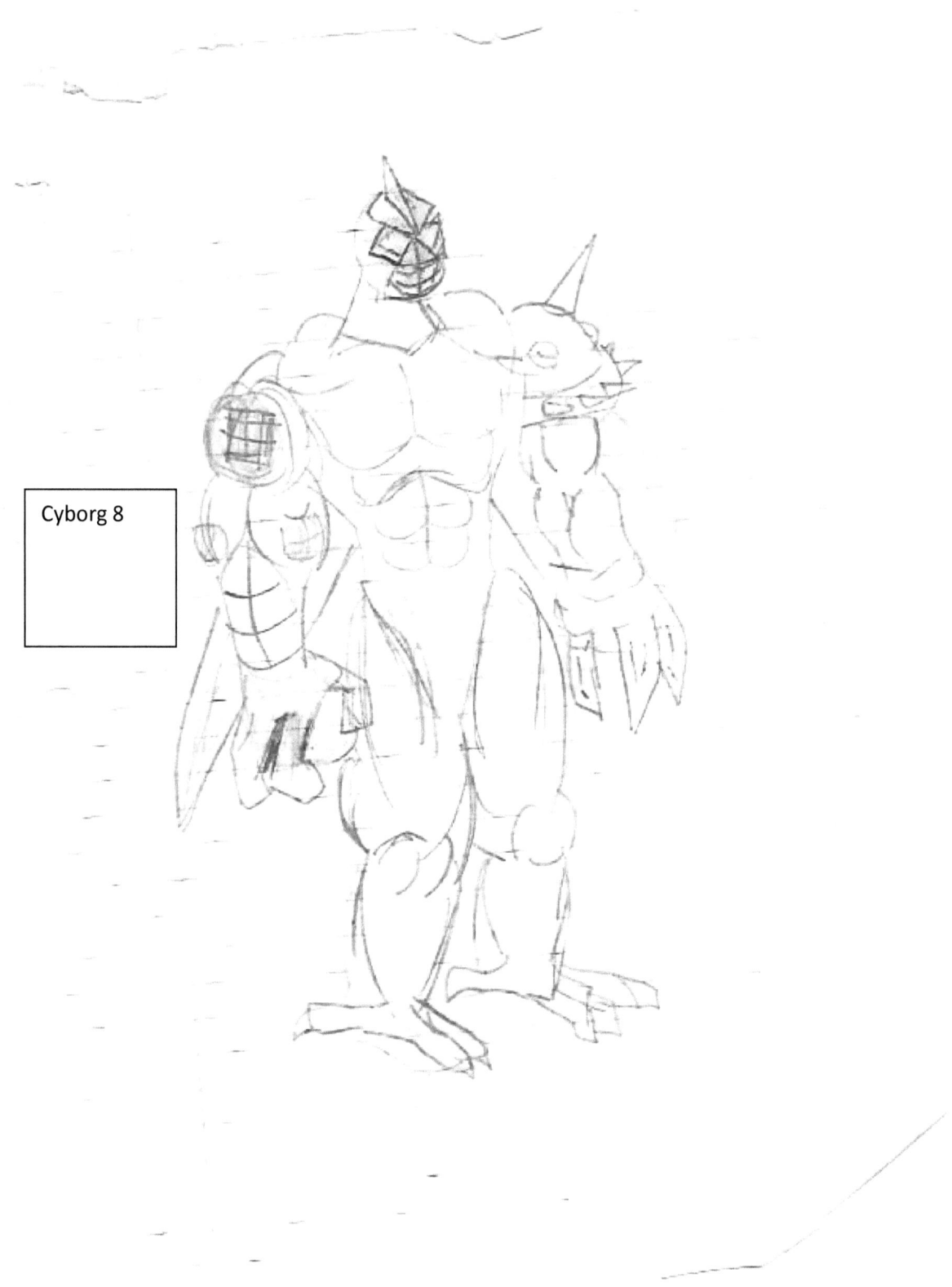

Cyborg 8

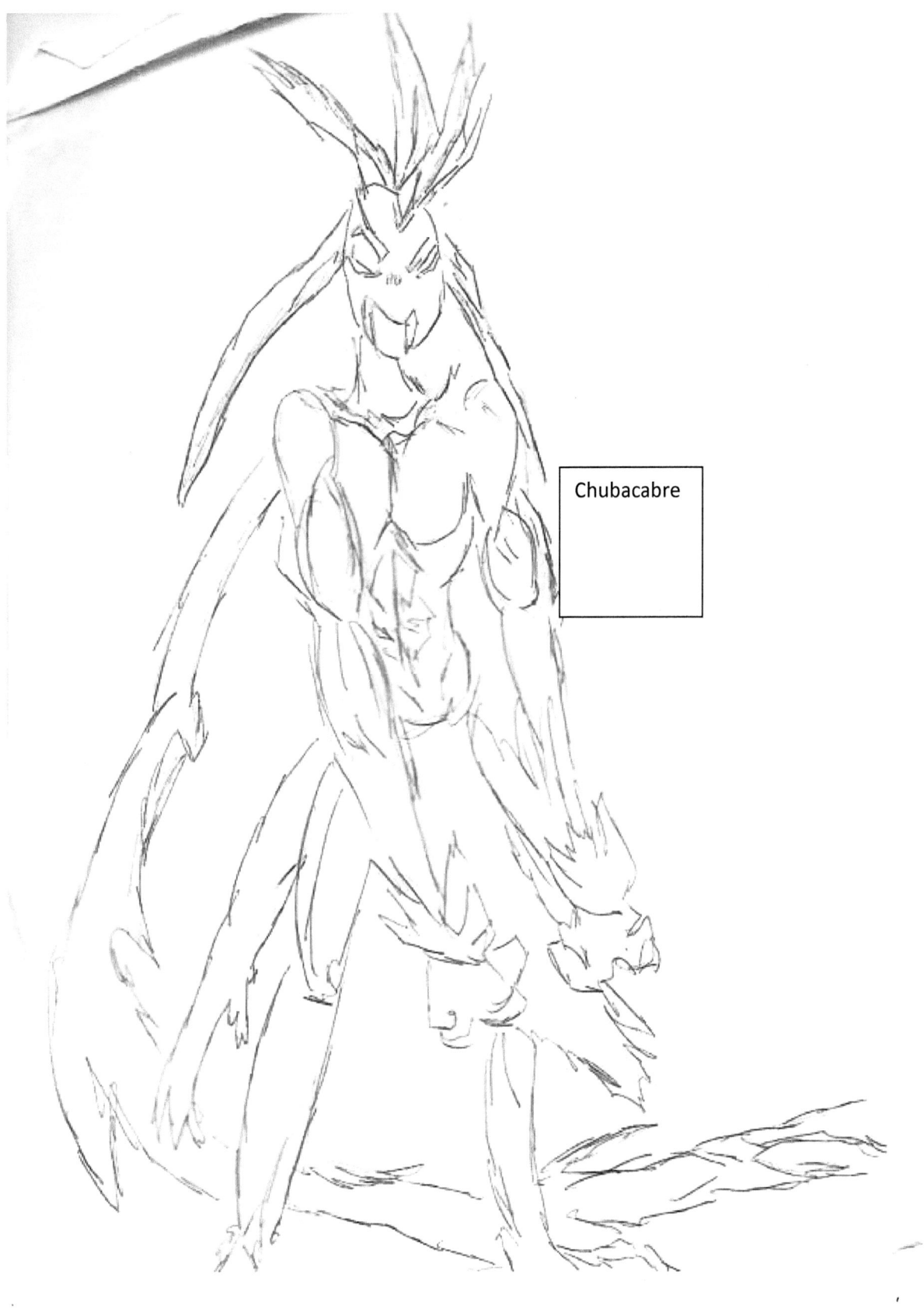

Chubacabre

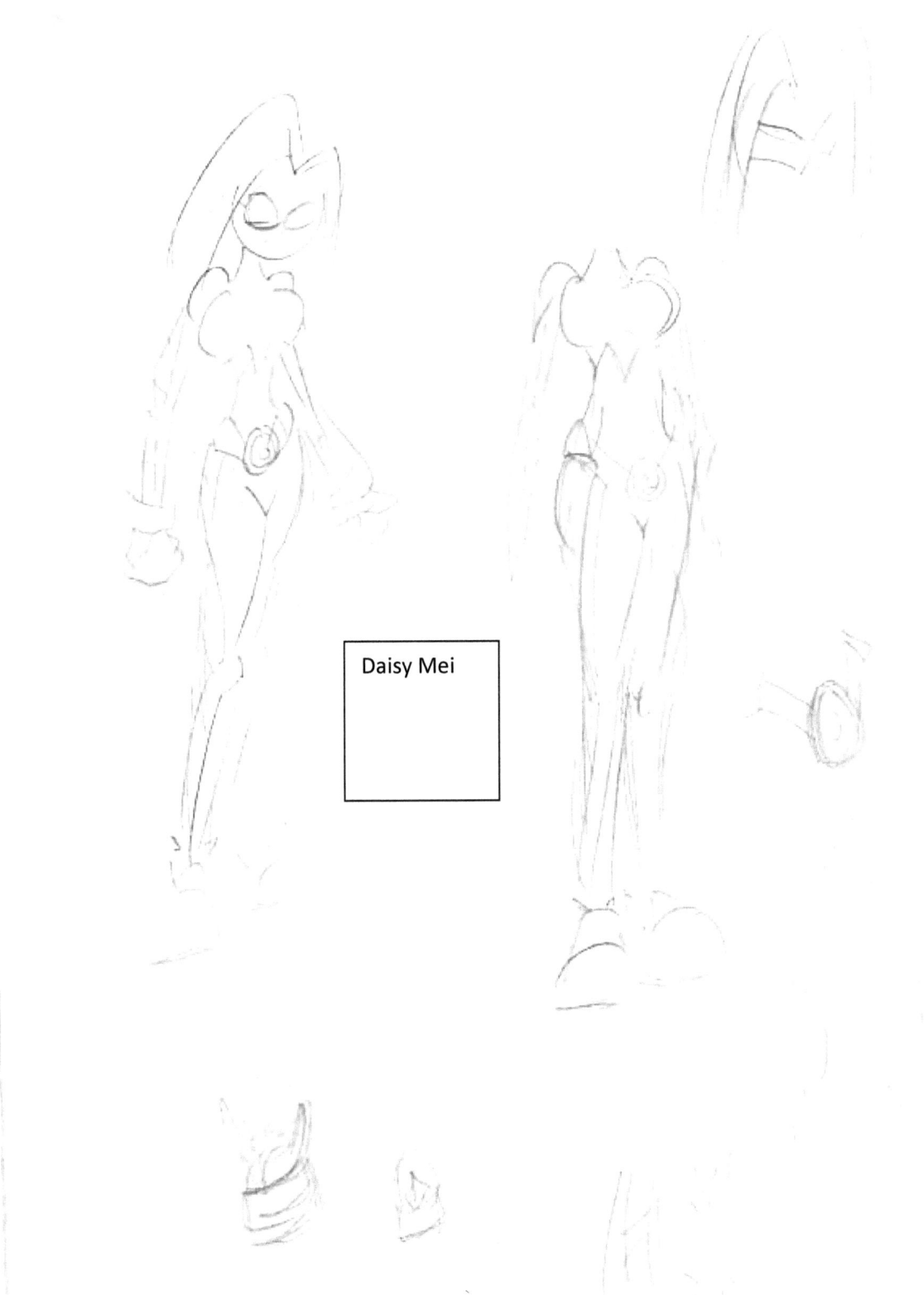

Daisy Mei

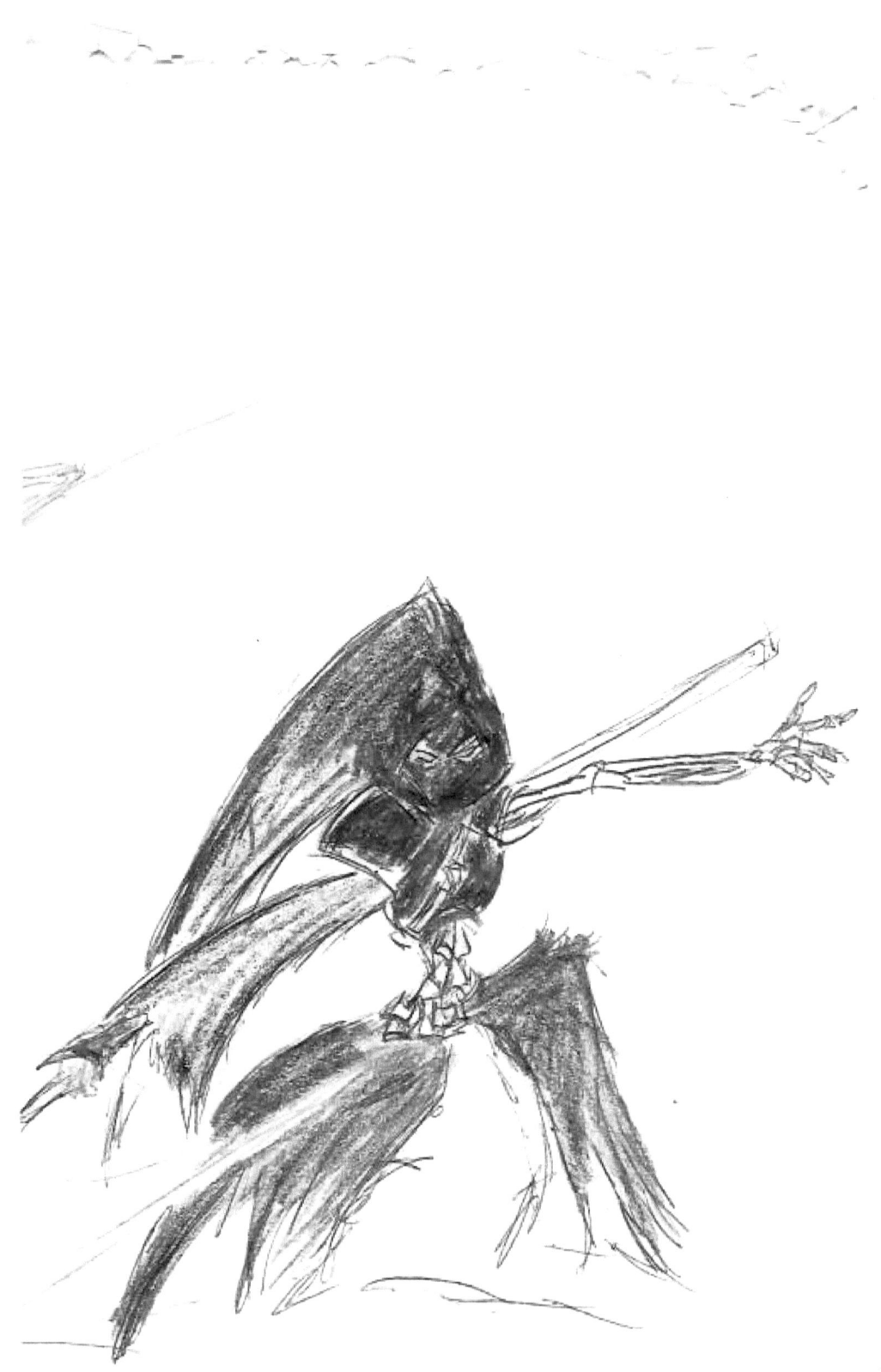

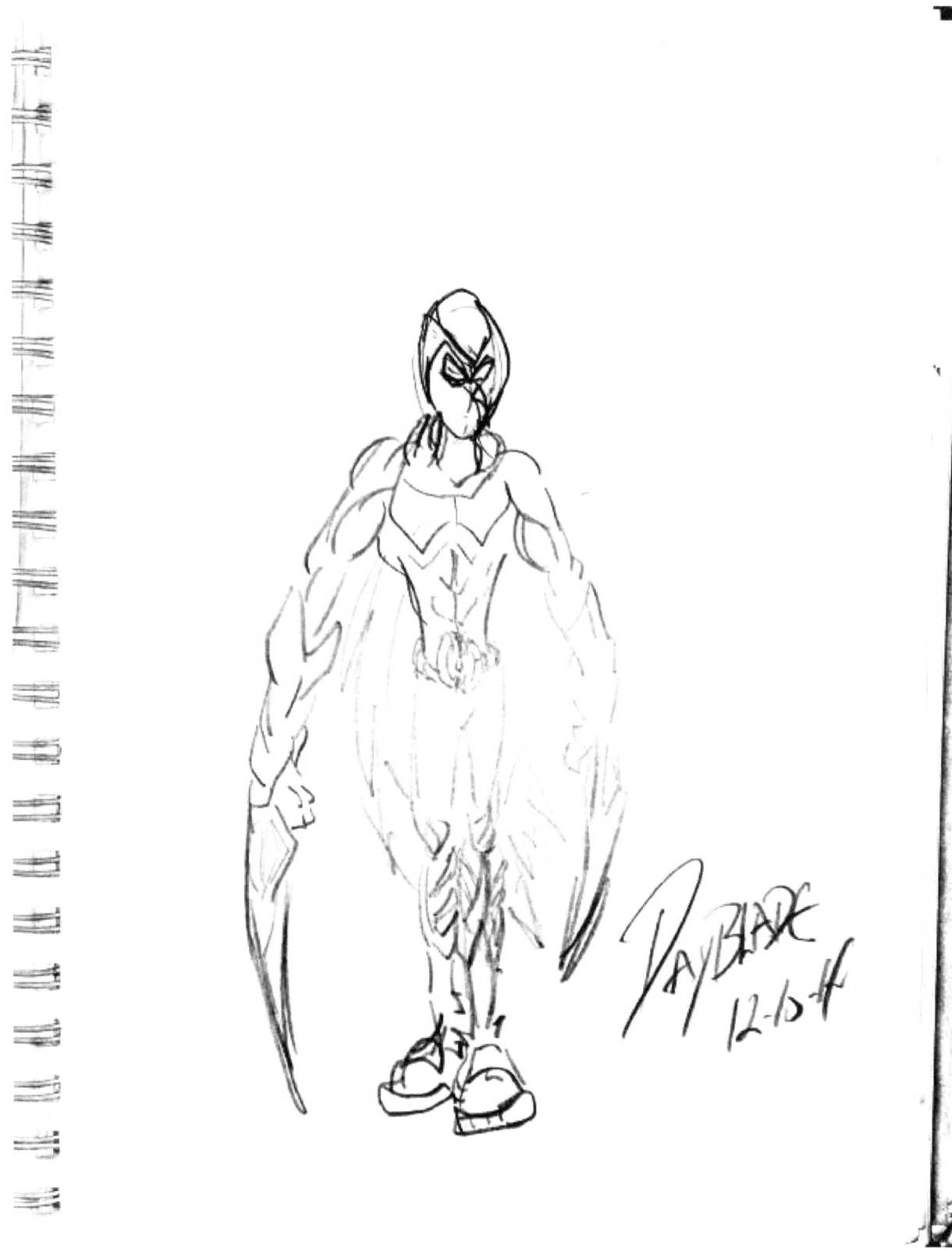

DAYBLADE
12-13-4

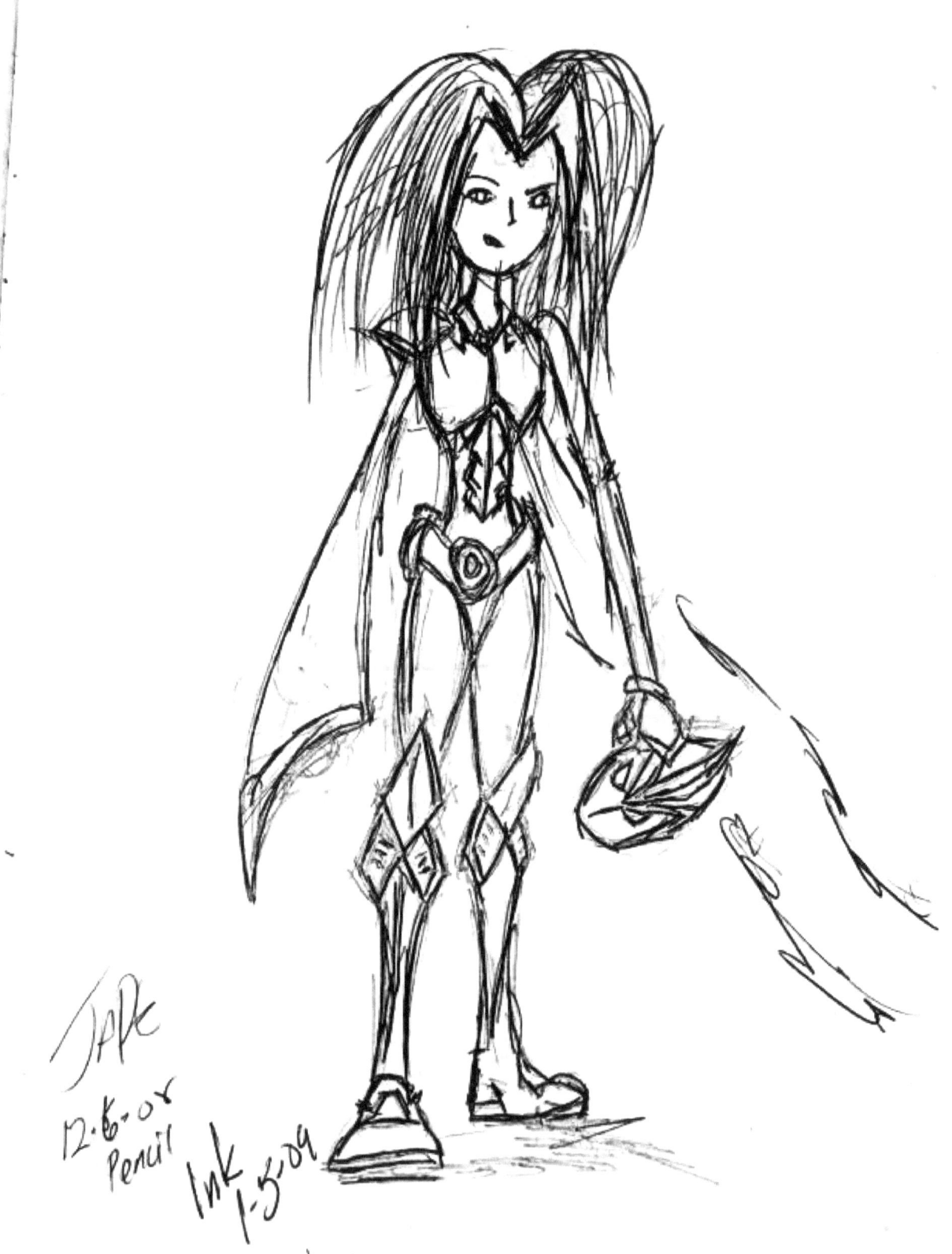

JAK
12-6-08
Pencil
Ink
1-5-09

40

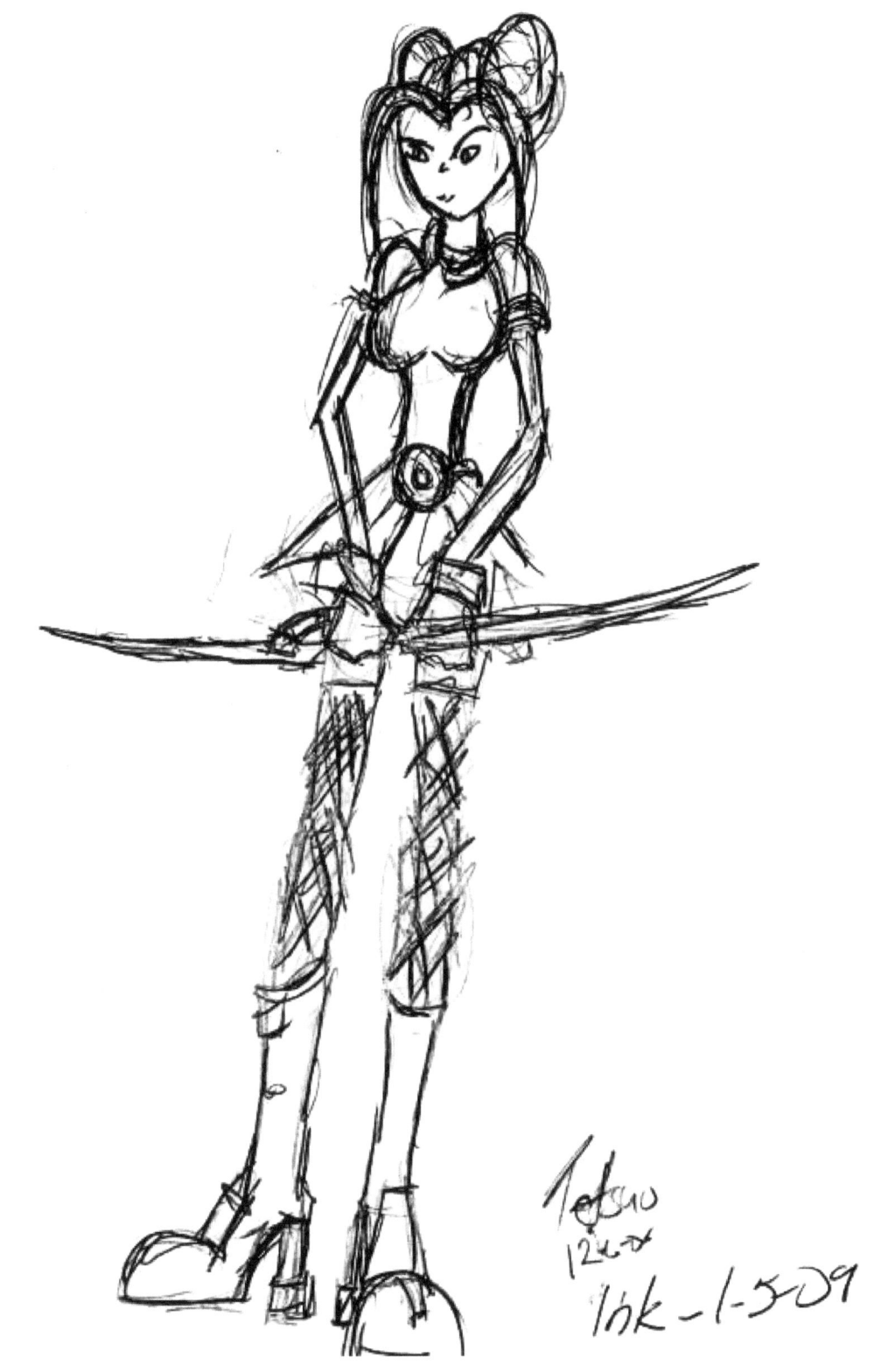

Tetsuo
12-6-08
Ink - 1-5-09

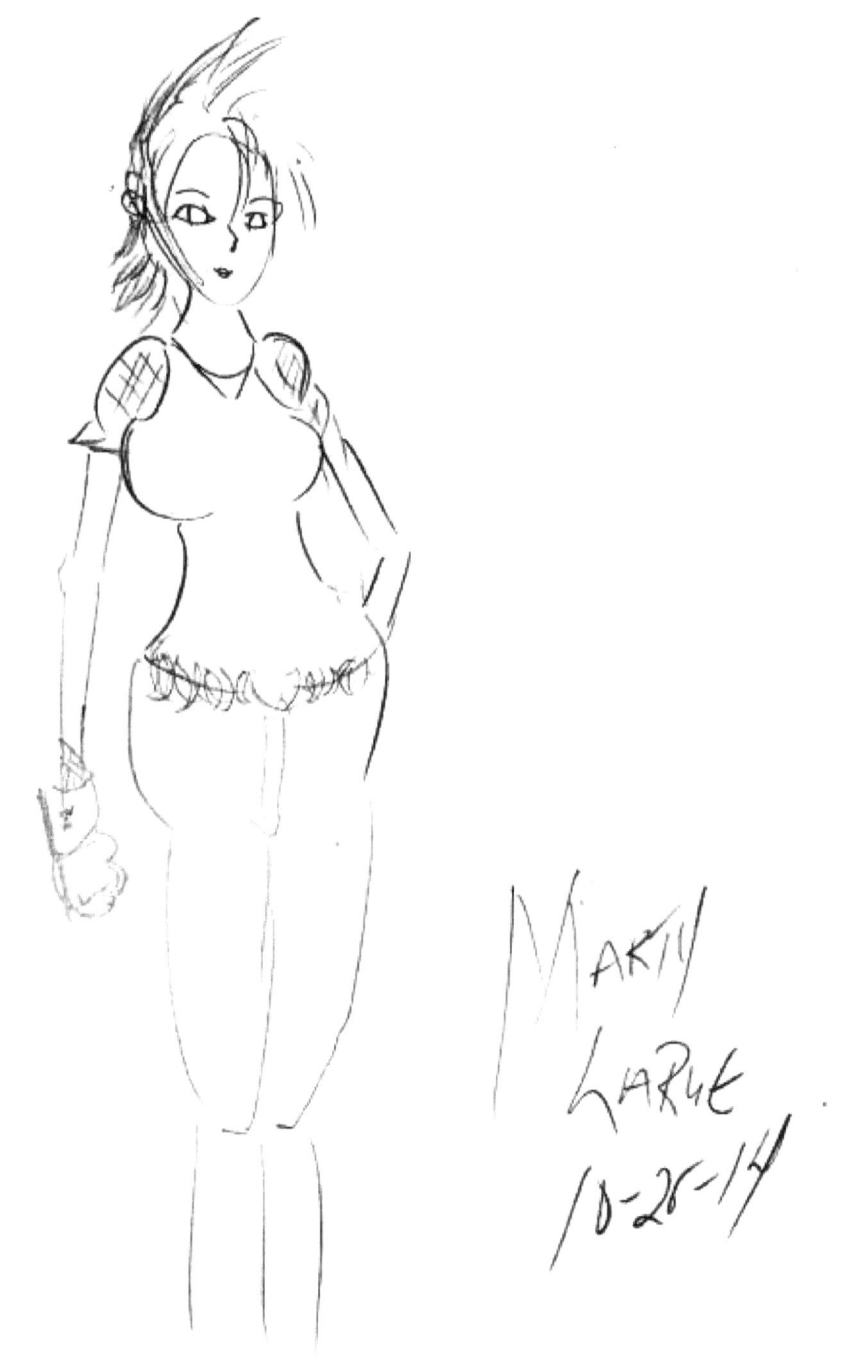

MARTY
LARUE
10-28-14

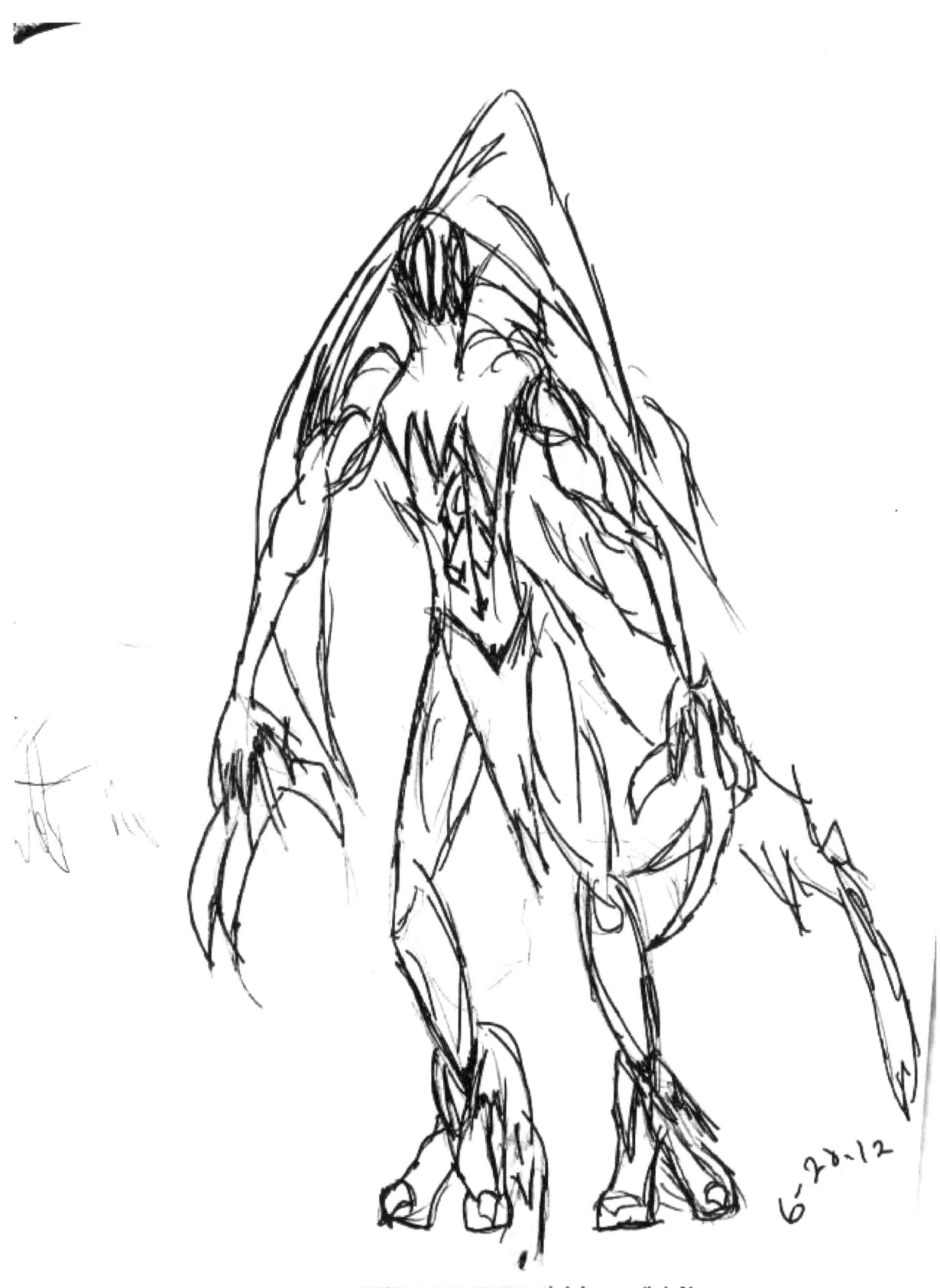

6-28-12

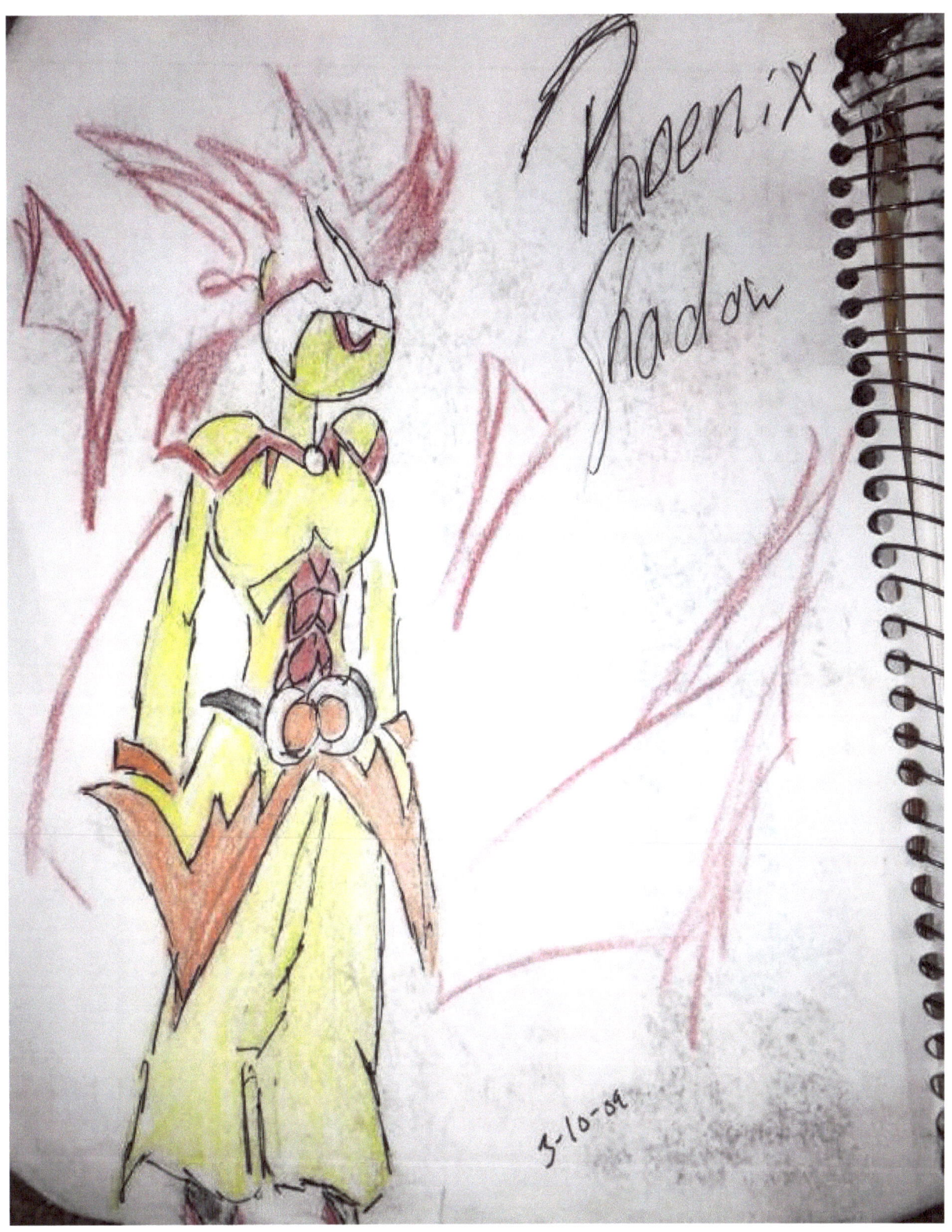

Phoenix Shadow

3-10-04

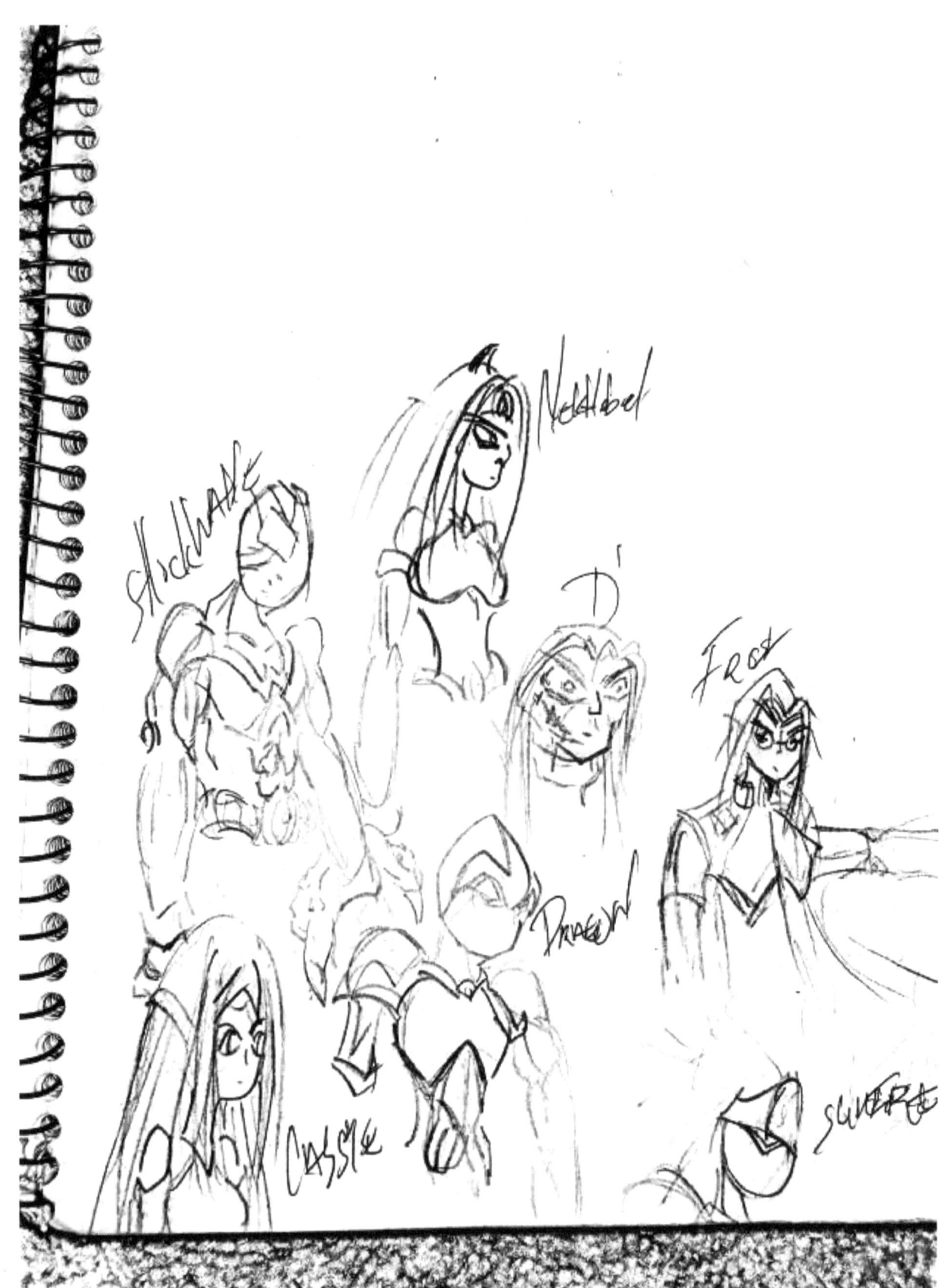

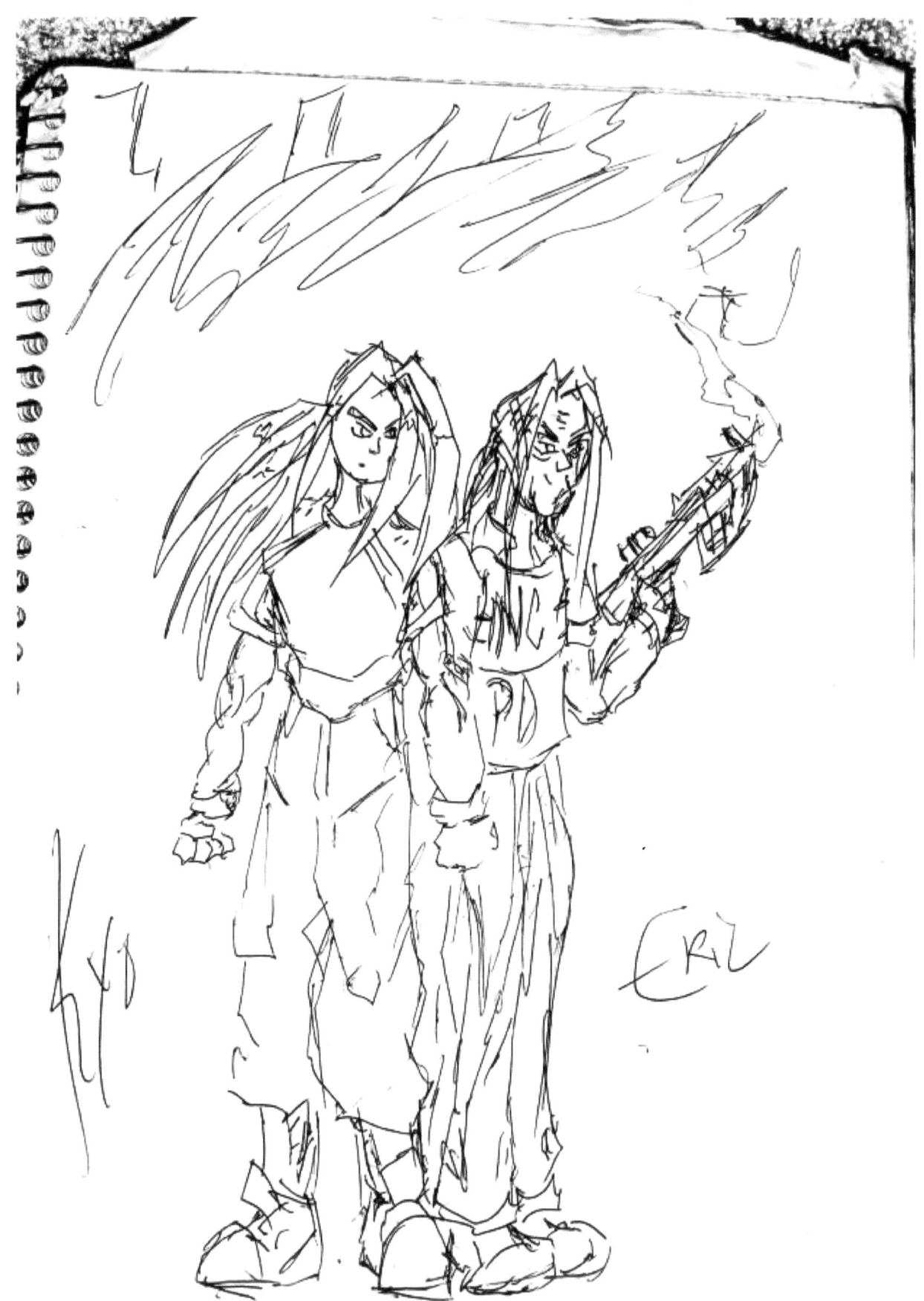

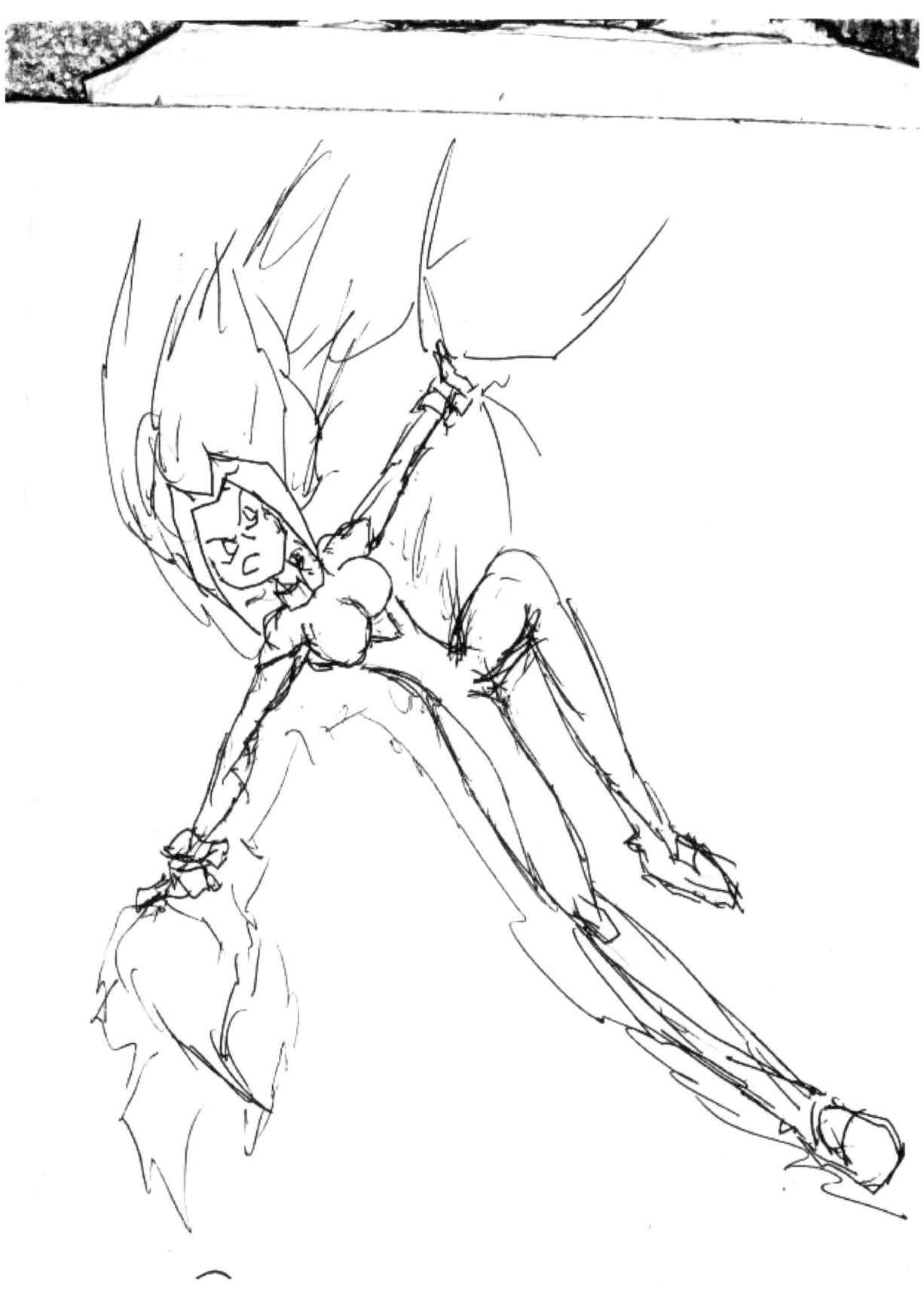

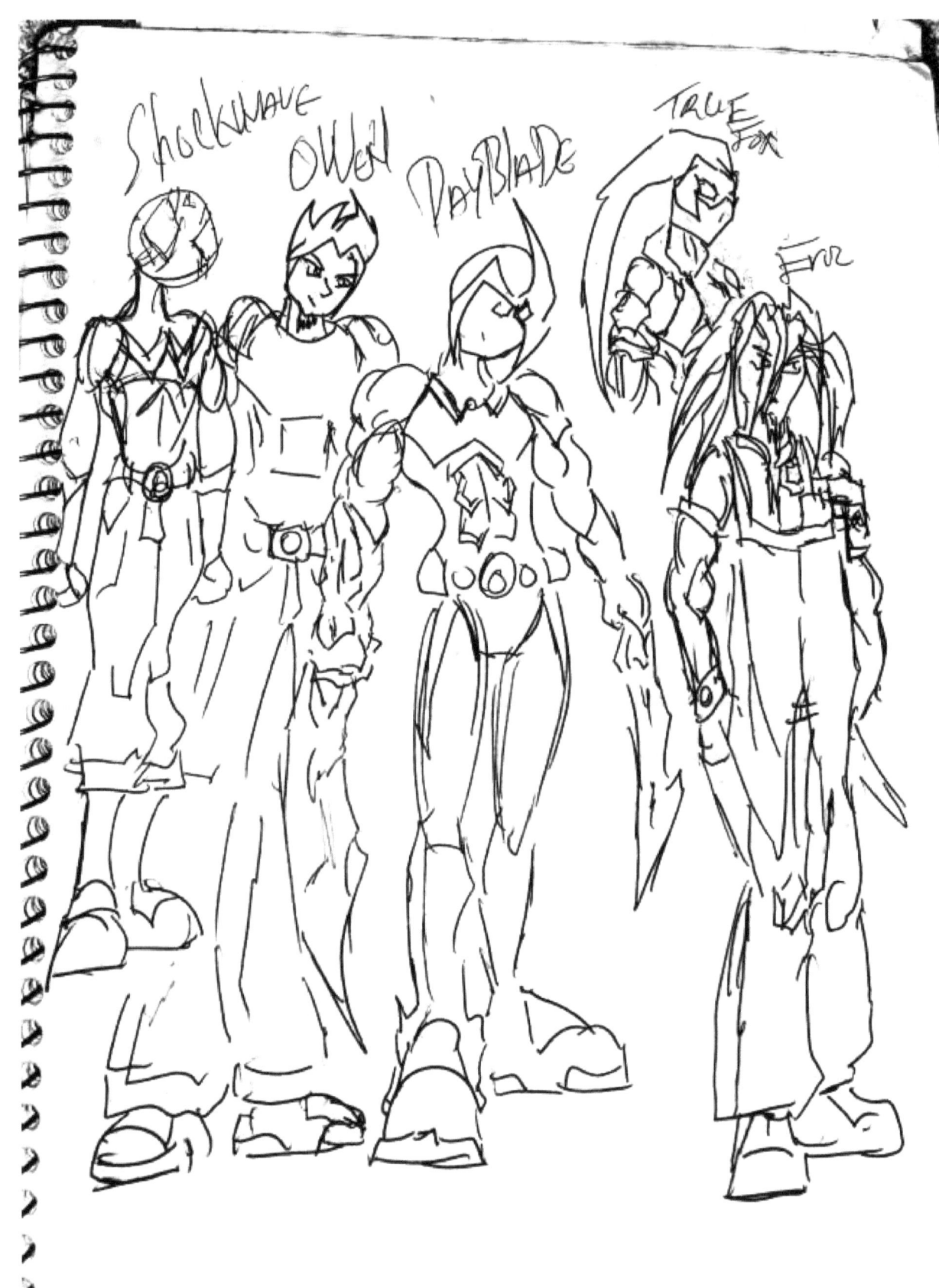

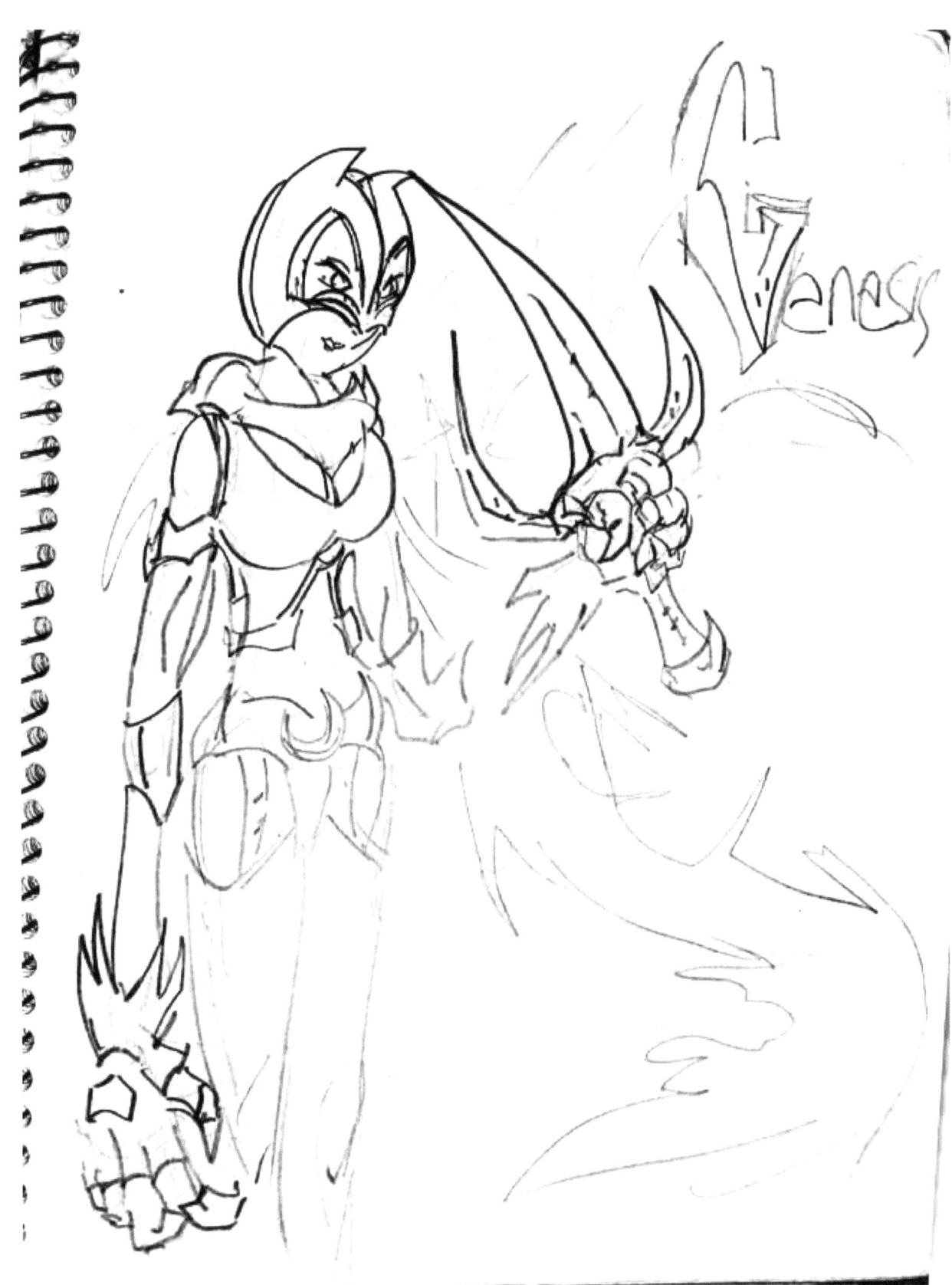

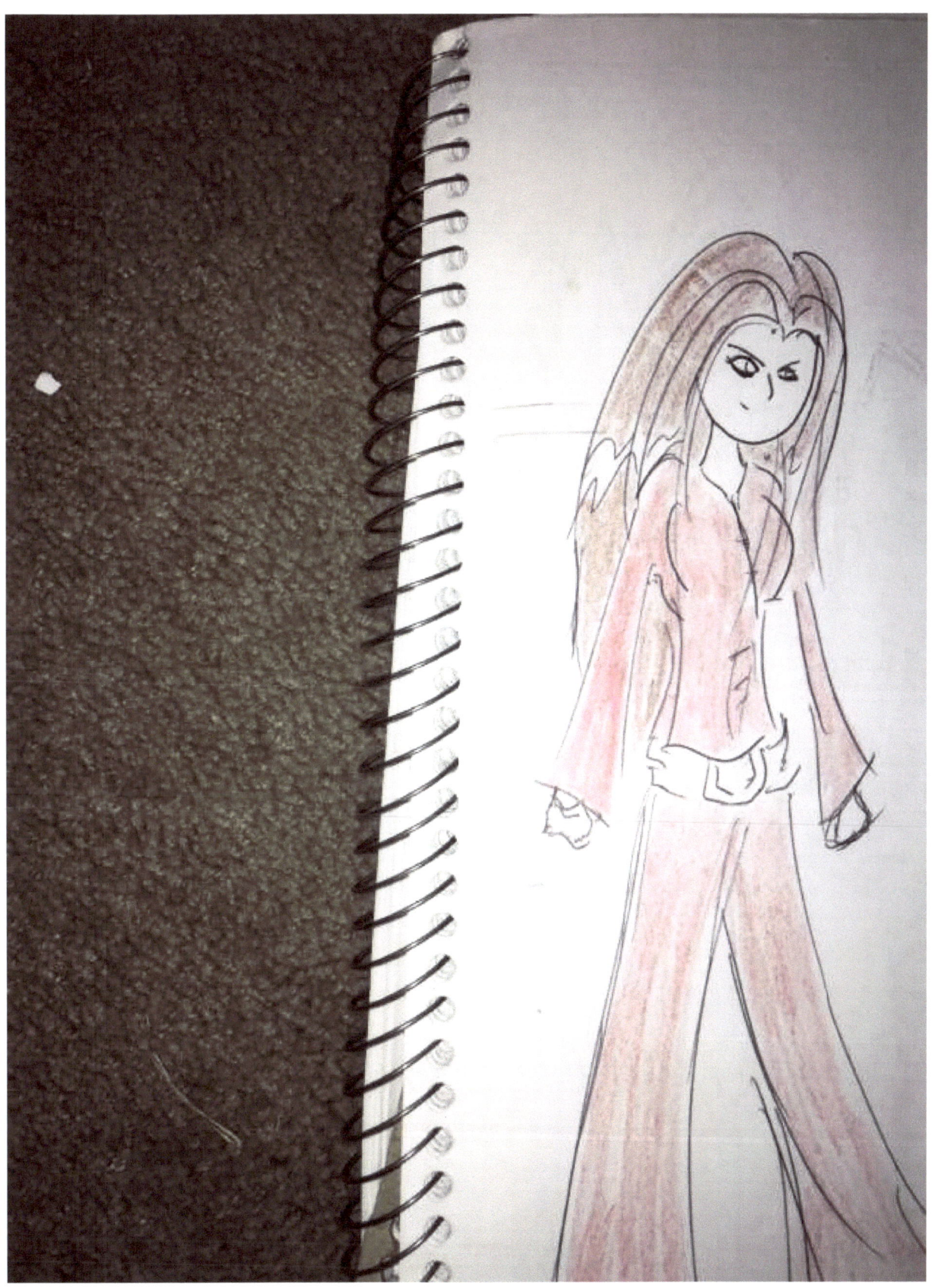

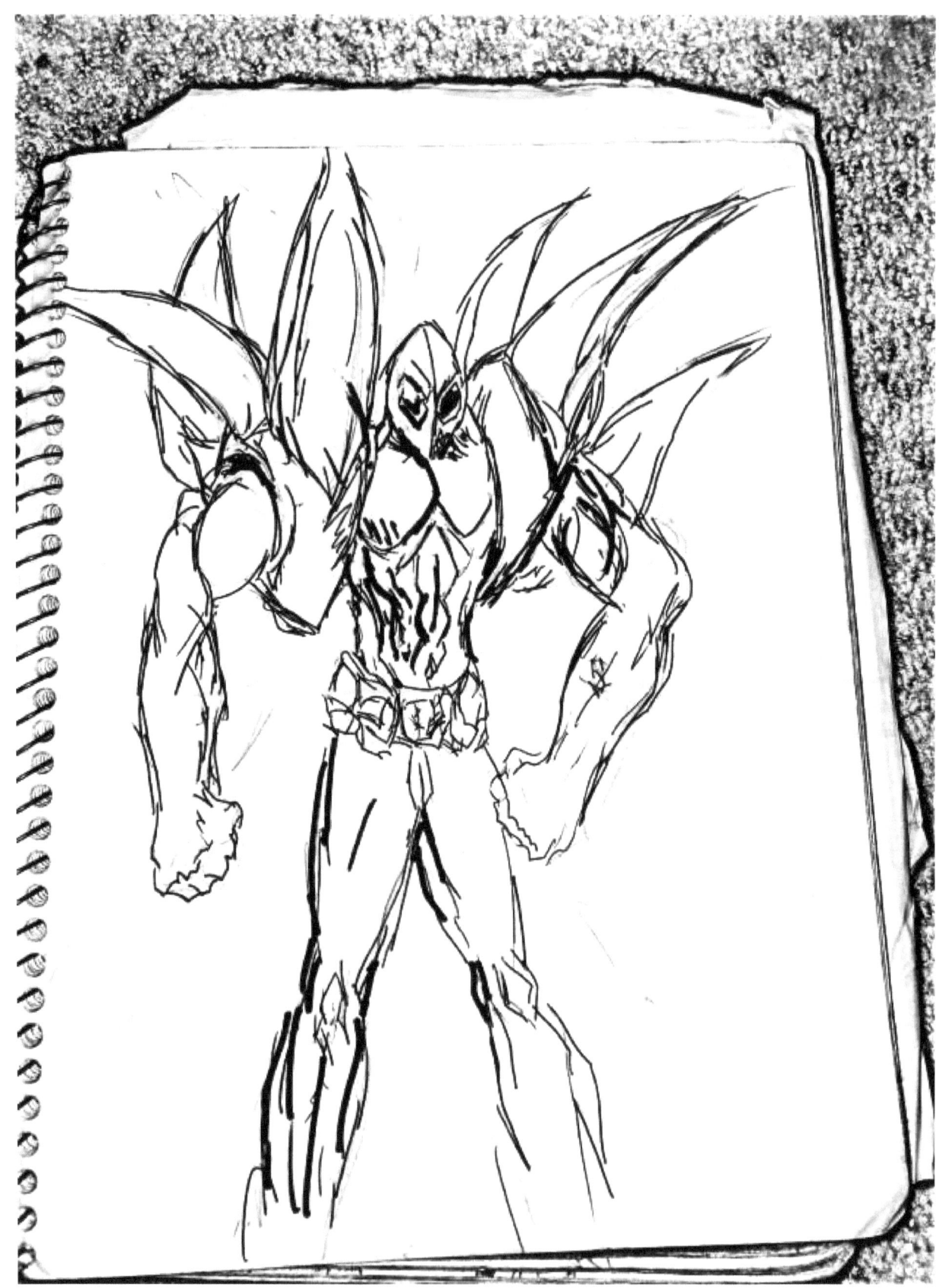

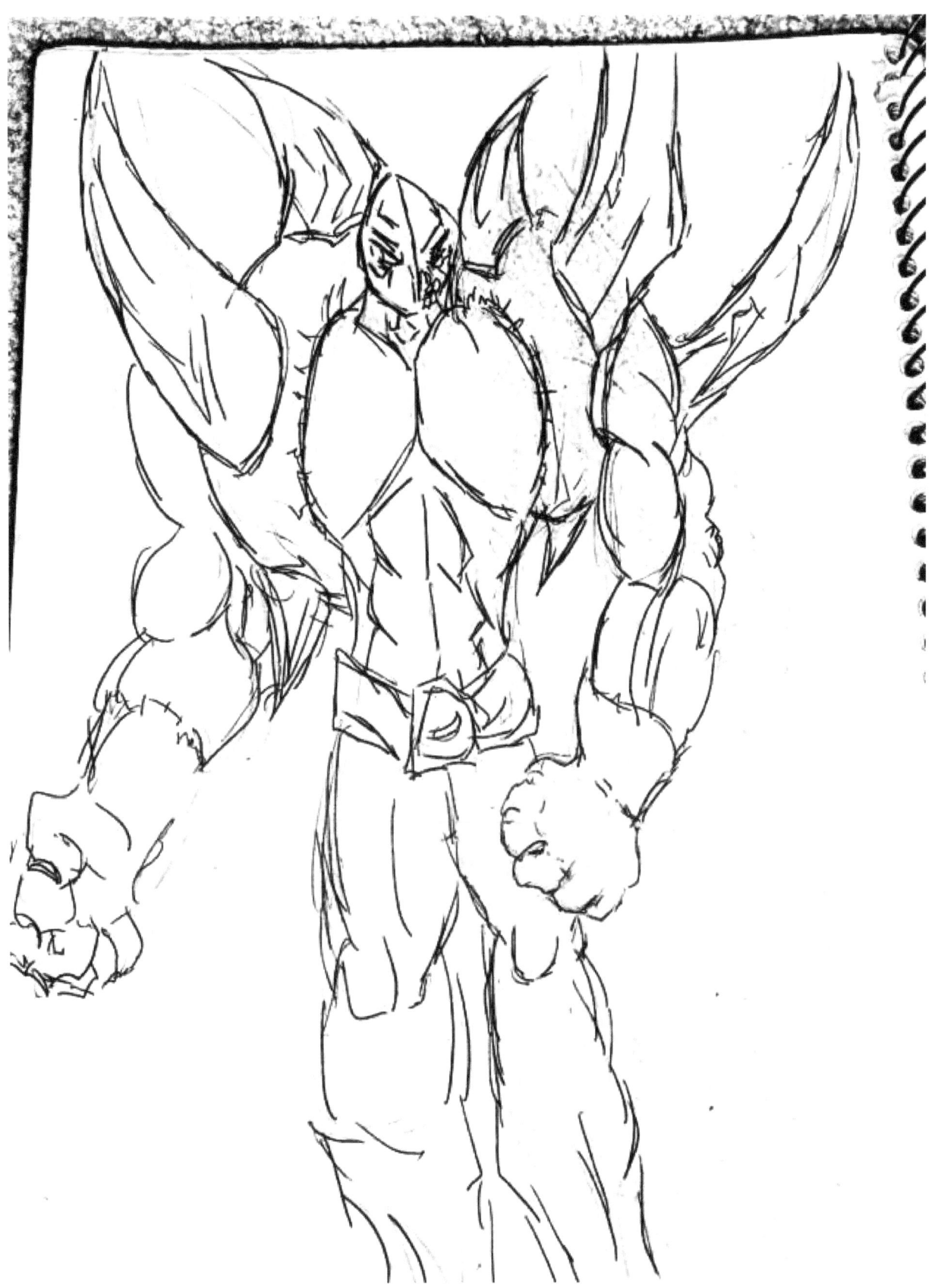

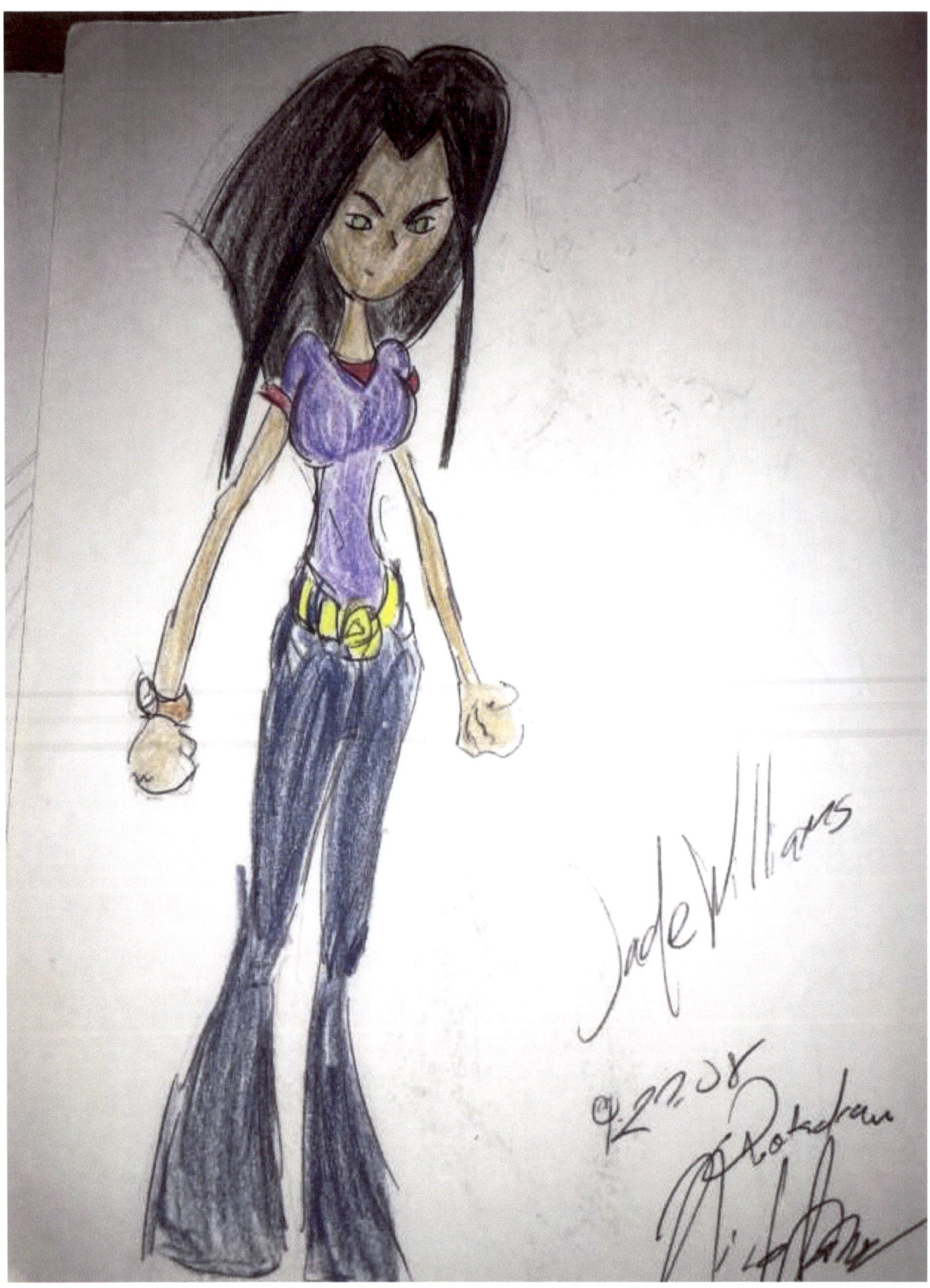

Jade Villars

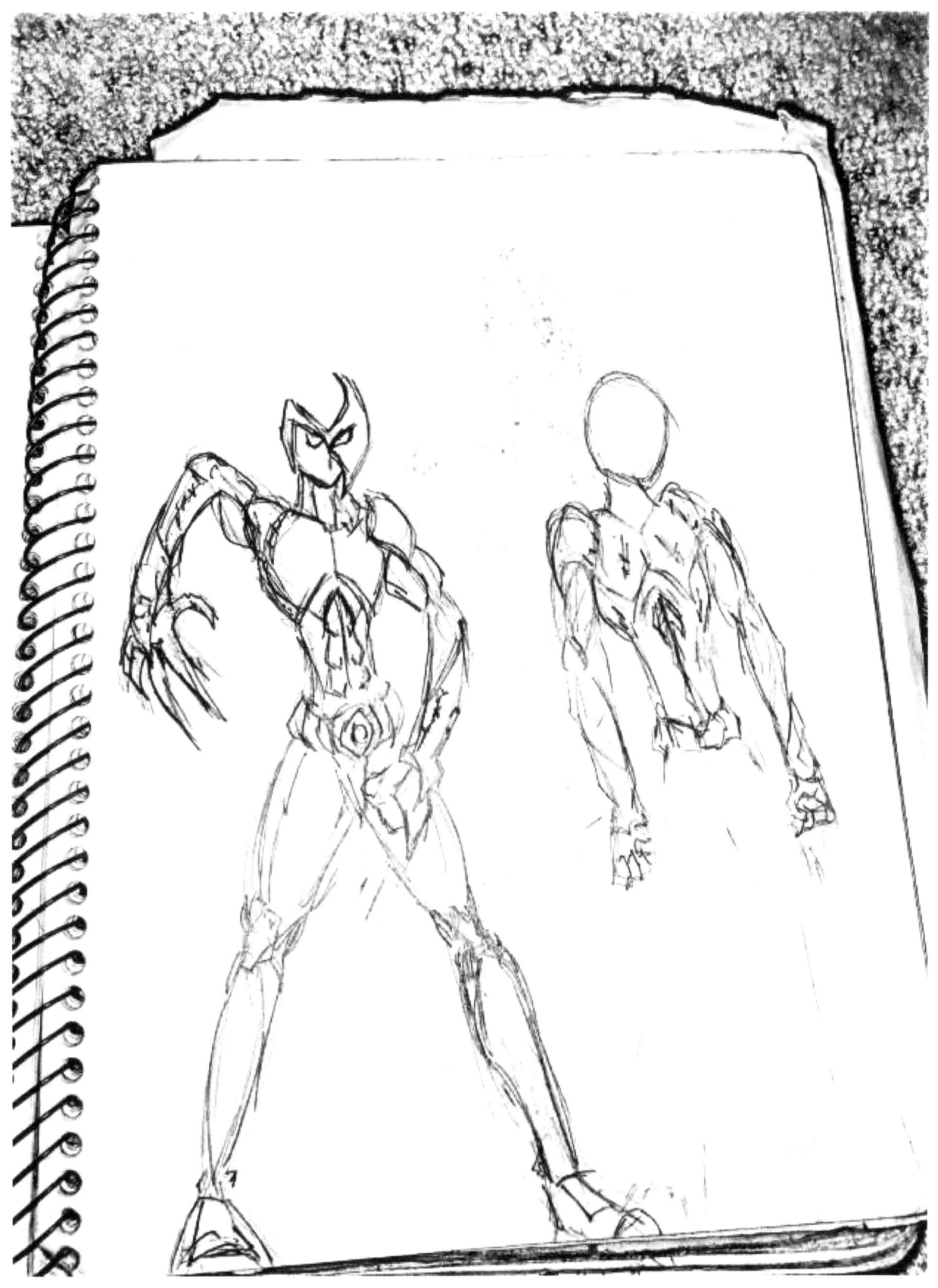

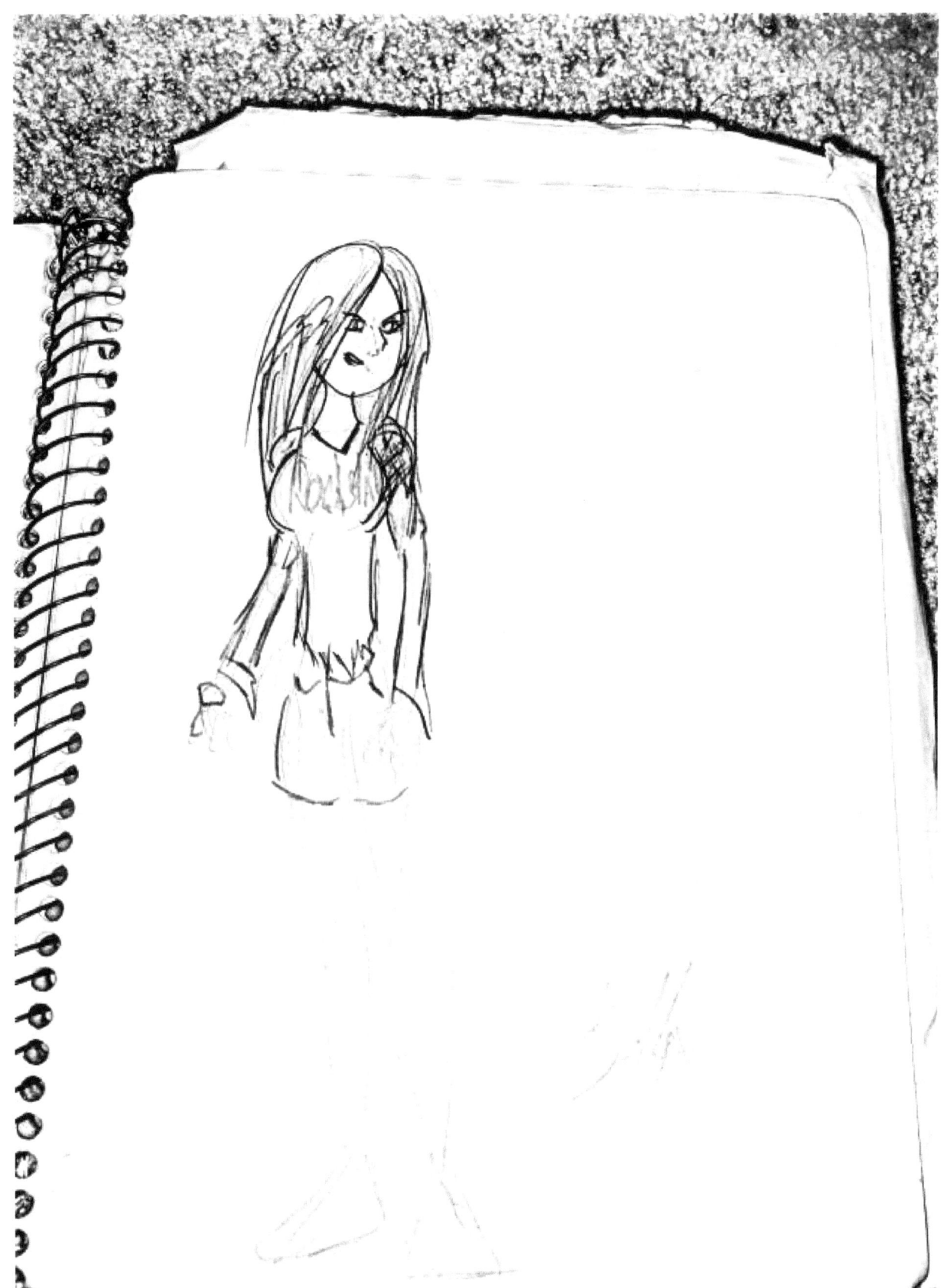

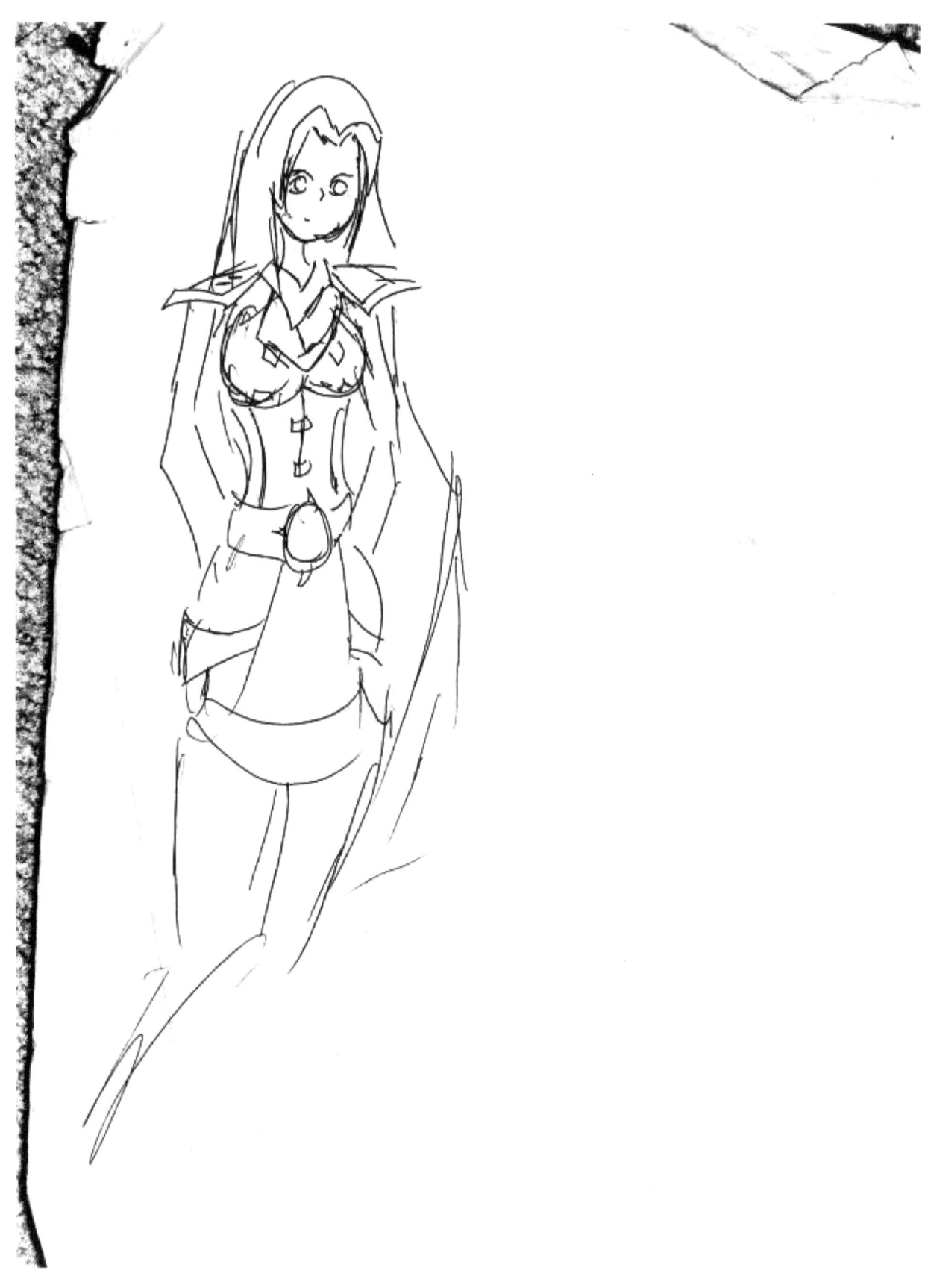

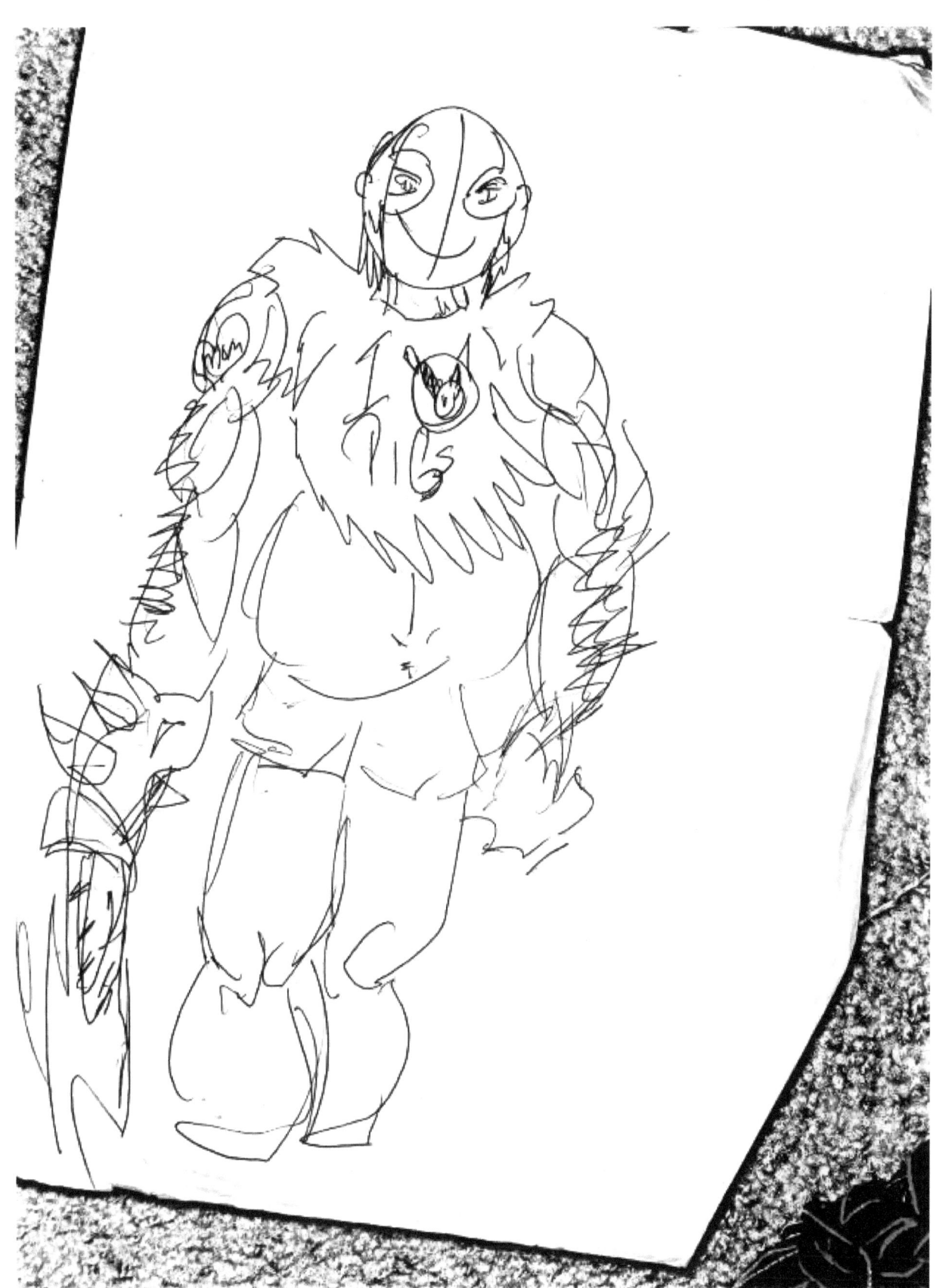

Heroes "Grim Reaper's Apprentices"

1st Aaliyah Jade – Egyptian Princess
2nd Arika Masamune – Japanese Ninja
3rd Senoj-Jin – Chinese Monk
4th Marie Oudete – French Paladin
5th Josalyn Ford – American Cowgirl

(sun) Sinbad = Sun Tribe Leader

 + Cleo'= Sun Tribe High Priestess

_____

Cassandra = Warrior Princess

Mihaku Sergio= Moon Warrior

 + Akira of Shihira

_____

Skylar (Moon)= Son of Moon Warrior, Jade's sensei. Tai (Dragon)= Dragon Moon Warrior

Sonia = star priestess

 + Skylar

_____

Summer and Sarah (stars)= sisters

Ken + Sophie = Kyi
Machine Masters

Tai + Sapphire = Kyo (Dragon)= Jade's rival

Sean, Monk Cet > Chico and Byron
Monks

(*source of inner powers or powers from birth)

WANDERS

K' = Timeless Best Friend of Kyo
J'mal

Simon Wilkes – The Witness

Raphael Pinkerton

Simeon The Soullifter

Andremda General + test tube
    Mark General
            + marries
    Mary Seadra

_____

Mantin General (GENOTRON) 1.

        2. SYNSYS (Synchronized Systems)
        3. King Coal and Energies
        4. Impression Records

Milton General (GENOTRON)
    Horsemen Corp
    Mountain Burgers

_____

Soul Creeper Family Tree

Nairobi Williams > Jade's biological Dad

"Tom" Jones > Jamal's Dad

Sergio Mihaku > Arika's Dad

Sinbad > Cassandra's Dad

Heather Williams > Jade's Biological Mom

Dawn Jones > Jamal's mom

Akira Shihara-Sergio > Arika's mom

Cleo > Cassie's mom

Drake Williams > Jade's twin brother

Ava, Ero, M-4 > Jamal's ½ siblings

Chang Shao > Arika's brother

J'mal > Cassandra's Brother

Nairobi + Heather = Jade & Drake

Tutan "Tom" + Dawn = Jamal

Mihaku + Akira = Chang Shao & Arika

Sinbad + Cleo = J'mal & Cassandra

Bosses & Rivals

Mantin General, Sr. owns Genotronics, SYNSYStems, King Coal and Energies, & Impressions Records
Milton General owns Mountain Burgers and Horsemen Security Corps.

Ash is CEO in GENOTRONics and King Coal

Daisy Mei is CEO is Water and acquired Gas from Nicole V.

Nicole V. eventually takes control of Impression Records.

Mantin/Jade, Arika, Cassie
SYNSYS/Eric Frost
King Energies/ Jade, Arika, Cassie, Jamal
Impressions/Drake, D', Ravillain X, DPS

Schools

Wildcat = animal

Pioneer = man

Warrior = heroes

Yellow jacket = animal (insect)

Hi Tech School = Career

Hero + Angel

Sinbad + Noel
Aaliyah

Arika + Atticus
Mihaku Sergio + Na'rob'i

Marie Oudete
Tetsuo + Lee

Josalyn Ford   Aaliyah

Jade Williams -------------

Noel – ghost

Atticus – cursed
Na'rob'l – scarred

Lee – silence

Aaliyah

Origin of inner peace

Noel /water

Na'rob'i/ desert

Atticus/moon

Senoj/desert

Lee/silence

Sinbad + Aaliyah/Sun

Mihaku Sergio + Akira/moon

Ash/chaos

Marie Oudete/stars

Tiffani Lopez/guidance

Kristy Jordan/knowledge & Wisdom

Joss Ford/Luck

Drake Williams/gifted

Jade Williams/Soul

Skylar/self-taught

Romantics	Kings
Aaliyah	Sinbad
Arika	Mihaku
Marie	Seth
Josalyn	
Jade	Drake
Rolnin students	
Sinbad, Mihaku	
Deadra's Students	
Trinity, Noel	

Students	teacher
Summer Star	Atticus
Sarah Star	Atticus
Jamal	Akira

K' Skylar
Kyle Tai
Kyo Tai
Jade Skylar

Sarah, Summer, Jamal, K', Kyle
    Atticus

Lynx, Cleo
    Fang

Sinbad, Aaliyah
    Noel

Akira of Shihara aka Spider, Dayhawk,
    Fang

Skylar, Tai
    self

K', Kyle
    Skylar & Tai

Owen, Eric
    Nigel

Cassie and Arika
    Jade

Heroes	Villains
S&S, Fox, Blaze: All	Mantis
Foxes	Chubacabre
Shadow	Psychoskull
All	Hunters
Skylar	Ash
Shadow	Nicole
	Daisy

Teams

Shockwave, Blaze, Fox, Spider aka Arika Masamune

NightBlade, Fang, DayHawk, Spider

Shadow, Shockwave, Kyo

Tai, Kyle, Kyo, Jin, Jade, Drake

Ash and Atticus

Rolnin, Marcellouis
Day, Night

Celestia, Trinity, Deadra, Noel

Sinbad, Sergio, Skylar, Sonia

Grim, Jade, Arika Masamune, Princess Cassandra

Sun Warriors
Story Treatment
(Cassandra)

Moon Knights
Story Treatment
(Arika Masamune)

Star Queen
Story Treatment
(Marie Oudete)

Spirit Warrior
Story Treatment
(Josalyn Ford)

Soul Creepers
Story Treatment
(Jade Williams)
Volume 1: New Girl On The Block

1) **Jade dies while Grim is trying to fight PsychoSkull. Rachel, Bret, Mantin, Owen, Kyo introduced.**

2) **Jade goes on an Afterlife tour with the Grim Reaper. Meets Saints, Angels, Demons,**

and Guardians of both Heaven and Hell. Grim Reaper tells Jade about the Hunters and PsychoSkull and his duty as Reaper. Jade's friend try to get Jade's fallen body to EMTs.

3) Jade returns to life after Reaper reveals her destiny to be with the Reaper's Shadow. Jade's friends are surprise that she survived being almost stabbed to death. She just tells them "That she's a very blessed individual."

4) Jade gets adjusted to having a new powers.

5) Grim reaps a dying woman's soul. Boyfriend kills himself to get a chance to fight the Reapers for her soul. Jade decides to take up the fight.

6) Mantin Sr. decides to use Mantin Jr. for a Hunter Project (M.A.N.T.I.S.), and unleashes him against the Reapers.

Volume 2: The Hunt Is On

7) Jade, Rachel, Bret and Owen decide to take a trip to Mexico for Spring Break. People are dying because of monsters called Chubacabres. These monsters are too much for Jade and Grim to handle so they get help from Cassandra, The Princess of The Sun Tribe.

Volume 3: Bring The Noise, Feel The Pain

8) Neo Cuidad hosts a battle of the bands. Hunters attack concert goers. Dead Poets, The Gurus, Leah & Isabella Carpenter make guest spots. Ravillain X's soul contract with The Devil comes into play. He becomes Satan's DJ.

Volume 4: The Worst Week Ever

9) Hunters start to target key souls. "The Immortal Swordsman"Revan Darkstar, Eric Frost introduced.

10) Hunters send assassins after Jade. Assassins attack her during a family reunion.

11) Jade and Grim are overtaken by Assassins, Hell's Musician, Psychoskull, War and Conquest (2 horsemen who work for the Hunters out of Boredom)

Volume 5: Reclaiming Our City

12) Hunters take control of Neo Cuidad completely. Crime shoots through the roof. Jade and Grim still recuperating. Eric Frost, Revan Darkstar try to fight against the gangs but barely have any affect. Owen is mortality wounded. Kyo dies. Bret tries to move in on Jade but she tells him, she can't love him back. Brett builds a battle suit.

Volume 6: The College Years

13) Jade focuses on school while still reaping souls.

Volume 7: The Beginning of the End

14) The main focal key is brought to the Hunter's attention.

15) The Hunters have almost acquired enough souls to release Marcellouis

16) Hunters send Psychoskull to take out the Immortal Swordsman

17) Hunters search for the 7 to help find Haiven

18) Hunters finally Confront Haiven

19) Hunters commit mass suicide and march onto Hell to release Marcellouis

Volume 8: The Horse Men

20) Pestilence
21) Conquest & War
22) Famine
23) Death

Volume 9: The End

24) Haiven and the Gatekeeper fight out of Hell. Tell Heaven about the release of Marcellouis and the reunion of Hell's Army. Jade decides to team with new allies

Finale: Good Vs Evil
All out Battle for Earth and humanity

Epilogue

Story Arches and Plot Lines: Shadow (Soul Creepers)

Prologue: The Birth of The Hunters/History of the Grim Reaper

    I.   Good vs Evil
    II. Banishment and Punishment
    III. Hell's Cult
    IV. Hell's Assassins
    V. Birth of Psychoskull
    VI. The Grim Reaper

Issues 1-6: New Girl On The Block

    I.   Jaded
    II. Angel, Saints and The Gatekeepers
    III. Reincarnation
    IV. Jade Learns 2 Drive
    V. Suicide Lover
    VI. A Father's Betrayal

Issues 7-11: The Hunt Is On

    VII. Spring Break Mexico
    VIII.   People of the Sun
    IX. Immortal Swordsman
    X. Hunted
    XI. Assassins Attack

Issues 12-14: Bring The Noise, Feel The Pain

    XII. The Battle of The Bands
    XIII.   Hell's Musician
    XIV.   Reaper Down

Issues 15-18: The Worst Week Ever

    XV. Bloody Sunday
    XVI.   Corporate Mercenary
    XVII.   Officer Down
    XVIII.   Kyo's Death

Issues 19-22: Reclaiming Our City

    XIX.   Bret ♥ Jade
    XX. The Gang Wars

Issues 23-26: The College Years

Issues 27-32: The Beginning of The End

Issues 33-36: The Four Horsemen

Issues 37-39: The End

Plot Lines

Prologue: The Birth of The Hunters/ History of the Grim Reaper

Good vs Evil

God and angels vs Lucifer and demons

- intense

ends with God and the angels winning but a little damaged

Banishment and Punishment

God cast Lucifer and his army into Hell. Locks Marcellous deep inside Hell.

Hell's Cult

Satan appears to a man and tells him to start a cult to find the key that locks away his general

Hell's Assassins

The cult grows stronger and starts training recruits for more in depth activity

Birth of Psychoskull

The cult starts to deal with dark arts and evil black magic and creates a guardian entity that can be resurrected through a different host body to ensure his soul will always survive through the ages

The Grim Reaper

The Grim Reaper recounts past battles of the millennia that just stick to his heart.

Issues 1-6: New Girl On The Block

Jaded

Jade dies during a battle between Grim & Psychoskull

Angel, Saints and The Gatekeepers

Grim introduces Jade to various angels & saints in the Afterlife

Jade is introduced to the Gatekeepers of Heaven and Hell

Reincarnation

Jade returns to life after she makes a deal with the Reaper

Jade Learns 2 Drive

Jade gets use to her new duties and tries to learn how to drive at the same time.

Suicide Lover

Grim reaps a dying woman soul. Dude kills himself to try to get her back. Jade intervenes

A Father's Betrayal

Mantin General Sr. selects his son to be the perfect subject for the Hunters new project.

Issues 7-11: The Hunt Is On

Spring Break Mexico

Jade and her friends decide to leave New City and enjoy a trip in Mexico. The Chubacabre unleashes on citizens of a small city. Grim sends Jade to investigate

People of the Sun

Jade -after losing fights to the Chubacabre finds aid from a monk sect located in the Mexican rainforest

Immortal Swordsman

The Hunters try to take the soul of a local shopowner in New City.

Hunted

The Hunters start to target key souls in their hunt to find the keys to release Marcellous

Assassins Attack

The Hunters take a contract on Jade's head

Issues 12-14: Bring The Noise, Feel The Pain

The Battle of The Bands

New City host a battle of the bands. The Hunters an attack at the concert goers and the performers.

Hell's Musician

Ravillain X, one of the performers from the battle of the bands dies. Goes to Hell. Makes a deal. Is reincarnated to aid the Hunters

Reaper Down

Jade and Grim are overtaken by the Assassins, Hell's Musician, Psychoskull and various Hunters.

Issues 15-18: The Worst Week Ever

Bloody Sunday

Satan appoints Ravillain status. Hunters wreak havoc on New City for a week. While Jade and Grim recoperate.

Corporate Mercenary

During the riot, Eric Frost decides to launch an one man assault against Genotron.

Officer Down

Owen is mortality wounded during the attacks and is forced to fight Ravillain for his soul.

Kyo's Death

Jade's love interest is killed she's forced to say goodbye

Issues 19-22: Reclaiming Our City

Bret ♥ Jade

Bret tells Jade how he feels. She needs time to think about. Bret reveals robotic battle suit to her.

The Gang Wars

The Gangs of New City decide to take the city after all the aftermath of the Hunters siege.

Streets of New City

Jade starts to fight living gang members in her reaper form, after she figures it's the only way to save the city

Jade's Loss

The Hunter's figure out Jade's identity and attacks her family at a family outing

Issues 23-26: The College Years

Jade focuses on school while still reaping souls

Freshmen

Sophmores

Juniors

Seniors

Issues 27-32: The Beginning of The End

Haiven

The main focal key is brought to the Hunter's attention

The Beginning of The End

The Hunters have almost acquired enough souls to release Marcellous

Psychoskull vs The Immortal Swordsman

Hunters send Psychoskull to take out the Immortal Swordsman

Journey

Hunters search for the 7 to help them find Haiven

The Key

Hunters finally confront Haiven

Liberating The General

Hunters commit mass suicide and march onto Hell to release Marcellous

Issues 33-36: The Four Horsemen

Pestilence

The 1st horsemen of the Apocalypse is released on the world

Conquest

2nd horsemen is released

Famine

3rd horsemen is released

War

4th horsemen is released

Issues 37-39: The End

Mortal Struggle and Conflicts

Haiven and the Gatekeeper fight out of Hell. Tell Heaven about the release of Marcellous and the reunion of Hell's Army. Jade decides to team with new allies

Finale: Good vs Evil

All out Battle for Earth and humanity

Epilogue